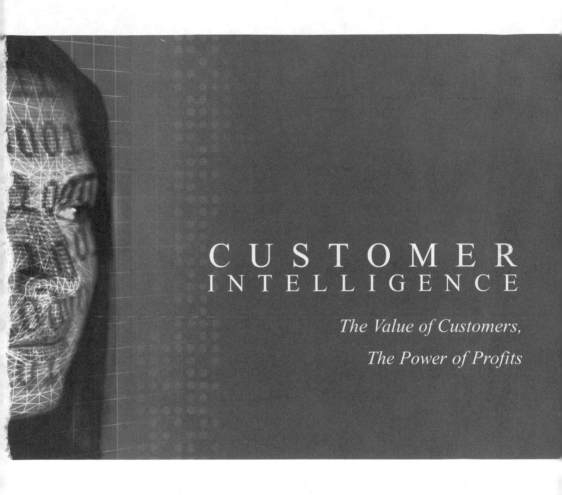

CUSTOMER
INTELLIGENCE

The Value of Customers,

The Power of Profits

GARY
HAWKINS

Author of

Building the Customer Specific Retail Enterprise

DEDICATION

To my wife, Heather,

and to my children —

Sterling,
Berkeley,
Schuyler
&
Haviland.

You are growing up too quickly.

APPRECIATION

I would like to extend my heartfelt appreciation to several people who have made my work such a pleasure…

My thanks to Mac and his team at M&M Meat Shops — you have been a wonderful group of people to work with. Mac, as I have told you many times, M&M Meat Shops is a special company. Thank you for asking me to be part of your team.

To Yamamoto-san and his team at Mitsubishi and Customer Communications — thank you for your hospitality during my visits to Japan, your patience and understanding as I have learned your culture, and most of all, your friendship.

My thanks also to Gary Friedlander and his team at Rice Epicurean Markets — your dedication to understanding and using customer information to improve your business, and to recognize and appreciate your customers, is inspiring.

And, lastly, my sincere thanks to the team at Green Hills — you are great.

CUSTOMER INTELLIGENCE
Copyright ' 2003 by Gary E. Hawkins

Cover design and layout by The WDBurdick Company.

Editing by Berkeley Whyte.

Library of Congress Control Number: 2003094934

ISBN: 0-9672562-1-6

Hawkins, Gary E.
CUSTOMER INTELLIGENCE

Published by Breezy Heights Publishing, P.O. Box 46, Skaneateles, NY 13152, United States
(US) 315.685.5175 / (www.breezyheights.com)

TABLE OF CONTENTS

There is at least one point in the history of any company when you have to change drastically to rise to the next performance level. Miss the moment and you start to decline.

Andrew S. Grove
Chairman, Intel Corporation

INTRODUCTION

For the better part of a century, since the venerated days of the corner grocer knowing his customers by name, retail strategy has revolved around products. From pricing to quality, category management to supply chain logistics, retailers have sought competitive advantage in product related activities. As these tactics yield ever-finer returns, competition has broached new territory, the shopping experience itself becoming the latest battleground.

But there's more. A small number of retail companies about the world are assimilating vast customer knowledge into their organizations, providing fertile grounds for the germination of new competitive opportunities. These pathfinders have learned that customer value must be viewed – and measured - in the context of years, even decades; not the transactional view of yesterday. Future success in retail will arise from the fusing together of not only product and customer based strategies, but a knowledge of branding and the value of time, all enabled by new technologies coming to market.

Gathering data from a variety of customer touch-points, world-class retailers are identifying massive amounts of their total sales to individual consumers on an ongoing basis, creating a veritable gold mine of information on customer shopping behavior. Such deep levels of information are used to enhance marketing, but more importantly, are being used to create definitive new measures of retail performance. Loyalty activities, such as improving customer retention or increasing shopping frequency, are but one subset of activities utilizing customer data in the customer intelligent company. This book is devoted to helping retailers become customer literate; devising new business strategies based upon using customer data to measure and manage retail.

First and foremost, customer information is a management tool. The elite of customer intelligent retail companies integrate customer data into their financial reporting, viewing through their income statements the different revenue and profit streams generated by their customers. Incorporating customer inventories into their balance sheets, these retail pioneers have the tools with which to evaluate their marketing and operational initiatives; such companies know if their efforts have served to increase customer purchasing, increase the number of customer households shopping with the company, or improved retention of valuable customers. Using customer-based metrics for benchmarking purposes, large retail companies have powerful new tools with which to monitor performance throughout their organizations.

Companies utilizing customer information now have a complete, holistic, view of their business, having accurate profit information relative to each product they sell and each customer that shops. These retailers are able to see, for the first time, whence their profits truly originate. Incorporating customer-based metrics into the company's management reporting, integrating product and customer data, these pioneers embed the understanding and use of customer measures into their company culture. By properly structuring the customer data, such information is used throughout operations, from marketing to merchandising, to improve decision making.

No longer viewing consumers as homogenous, these companies look beneath the surface of their total sales. Just as the oceans teem with different fish, so too do our stores with a diversity of customers. Utilizing available technologies to interact with consumers, retailers can now go to market on an individual customer basis, dramatically improving business performance. Such new capabilities at last sever retailers from the "one price for all" dogma that has been the sole province of efficient mass marketing.

The ability to measure consumer shopping behavior over time provides a dramatic change in perspective. Retailers in the past have had only a snapshot view of their customers; time was encapsulated to the transaction, the retailer not knowing if each transaction was a unique customer or the same customer returning. A select group of retailers have quietly built their knowledge base of customer behavior over the past decade; they have learned that there exists a highly profitable core customer constituency, one that is sometimes overlooked in traditional loyalty programs. In addition, these companies are now aware of the migrations of all their customer segments over time. Using customer-based metrics such retailers are able to bring a unifying laser-like focus to maximizing the lifetime value of their most important assets.

Hundreds of retail companies about the world, already possessing large quantities of customer data, have within their grasp the power to transform their businesses, yet it goes unused. Thousands of other companies let immense amounts of valuable customer data slip between their fingers each day. Many retail executives seem to understand the potential value of customer information relative to marketing, yet few significantly alter the way they go to market to capitalize on such opportunities. Very few executives have contemplated how detailed customer data can yield valuable new business measures. Retail executives, suffering from product myopia, have yet to discover the power of becoming customer literate.

In too many cases, it has been the availability of technologies that have pushed loyalty marketing and customer relationship management initiatives in retail rather than a comprehensive strategy driving the solutions enabled by the technologies. In addition, retail companies have been at a loss as to developing measurable return on investment figures related to their customer relationship marketing efforts. Hard metrics are needed to evaluate the results of these initiatives.

The fast-moving retail environment seems to breed tactical thinking, little thought given to long term strategy. And yet with rapid consolidation and channel blurring impacting most every retail sector, adopting such long term survival strategies is more critical than ever. In the hands of knowledgeable practitioners, customer information is a disruptive technology, altering the traditional rules of competition. All sales dollars are not equal; the retail battles are shifting from share of market to share of customer. Leading retailers are willing to sacrifice the least profitable consumers to their competitors, realizing that in doing so they can improve the value proposition offered their more valuable patrons.

This book is about creating new retail business strategies through an understanding of the multiple dimensions in which retailers operate; products, customers, the shopping experience, and time. These strategies require and reward a long term perspective when building and maximizing the value of a customer base; far different than the quarter-to-quarter financial frenzy driving many companies. No longer will linear thinking, doggedly pursuing ever-finer efficiencies in product logistics, and tactical execution of tired product price promotion win the day. This new world of retail calls for more creative leadership, people able to think beyond the single plane of product metrics. Now that we can measure these multiple dimensions of retailing, we must learn to conceptualize new strategies.

Retail companies comprehending these new paradigms can stake out fresh positions in their marketplaces. Through the integration of product and customer information, retailers are now able to truly align their operations with their customers, exponentially increasing the effectiveness of their business strategies. Vast opportunities await retailers, in a multitude of channels, who understand this new environment.

There are few companies that cannot benefit from greater knowledge and understanding of their customers. It is the rare business that cannot gain from improved economic measures growing from customer-based information. The concepts and practices of this approach to retailing are applicable across most channels. Indeed, we are seeing an explosion in the gathering of detailed customer information in channels such as supermarkets, hypermarkets, drug stores, discounters, bookstores, convenience stores, department stores, and niche and specialty retailers.

Using information gathered through retail frequent shopper programs, online shopping, proprietary payment cards, and others, leading companies are amassing vast repositories of customer behavior data. While this information is gathered through multiple customer touch-points, some retailers have evolved far beyond the basic tenets of loyalty marketing. A loyalty marketing program may be one component of a customer intelligent retailing strategy. It is an interface through which a retailer is able to gather customer information and influence customer behavior. One can practice loyalty marketing without practicing customer intelligent retailing; but one cannot become a practitioner of customer intelligent retailing without a customer interface. A loyalty marketing program is to a customer-integrated retailing strategy as wheels are to an automobile.

But with the power provided by vast levels of customer information comes responsibility. Privacy and confidentiality of data are issues that have reached critical mass in many countries around the world. Without doubt, the retail industry must make the confidentiality of such customer information one of their highest priorities, ever-vigilant that they not betray their customers' trust. To date the retail industry has done an exemplary job of protecting their customers' information, cognizant of the relationship they have. Wise retailers understand that having such knowledge provides for the recognition of their most valued customers, not the fiscal punishment of the deal-seekers.

Critics of retail loyalty marketing dismiss such programs as simple discounting schemes; what were once paper coupons are now electronic, obtained by the customer using their frequent shopper card; far too many retail loyalty programs are simply promotional gimmicks. Such critics are correct in many cases... but not all.

Others claim that traditional retail loyalty schemes are too costly; it is only necessary to gather information on the retailer's "best customers". Fee-based loyalty schemes purport to do just this, proclaiming that only "best customers" will pay the entry fee, receiving stated benefits for doing so. But, just as any merchandising-based strategy will falter if only having partial product sales data, having only a limited amount of customer data will not support a successful retail strategy bringing together both products and customers.

Many retailers around the world have established retail loyalty programs, are contemplating launching one, or are competing against one. This book will explain the strategy behind such programs and how they can serve as the springboard to a more powerful retail system.

For those retailers already involved in such efforts, this book will help revisit the reasons why they became involved in retail loyalty marketing in the first place. By tracing the evolution of frequent shopper initiatives over the past decade, retailers can see where they may have stalled, the tactics used by leaders in the field, and how they can further evolve their use of customer data.

For those retailers considering getting involved, this book provides a primer on evaluating the applicability of this strategy to various retail channels and what it takes to implement a world-class effort to gather, understand, integrate, and use detailed customer information in retail.

And for those retailers competing against such programs, this book will assist in providing a deeper understanding of what's really at stake, beyond the occasional marketing promotions.

So as to better understand the forces driving the creation of these new strategies, the book will begin with a look at the retail industry today and the major trends shaping retail. Next, we will build the case for gathering and using customer information, and see how such efforts can provide a true win-win relationship between a retail company and its customers.

Growing from this customer information, we will explore how leading companies are structuring the vast amounts of data they are capturing, facilitating the assimilation of customer knowledge into the company's operations and culture.

Using these new customer-based measures, companies have new ways to go to market and to evaluate their marketing endeavors, at last having a way to directly measure marketing's impact through changes in customer behavior. After examining the requirements for success, we will take an in-depth look at several companies using customer knowledge to underpin their business strategies. Lastly, the book explores the impact of new technologies coming to market and how they are at last providing the infrastructure for retailing to individual customers on a mass basis.

Throughout the book you will find real-world illustrations drawn from retailers in several channels from around the globe. Many of the examples are drawn from the supermarket sector due to the fact these companies have been at the forefront of using customer information in retail. Chapter Six is devoted to presenting case studies of three particular companies; M&M Meat Shops, Rice Epicurean Markets, and Green Hills, in addition to observations of an ongoing retail battle from an outside perspective.

M&M Meat Shops operates in a unique retail niche, selling only frozen food products. Having over 300 stores across Canada, M&M Meat Shops is a franchise company, each store individually owned but all operating beneath the M&M Meat Shops umbrella. The continuity offered by following the M&M Meat Shops story as their efforts have unfolded provides us many lessons, from viewing the obstacles and challenges encountered, to how to best make use of such a strategy at an individual store level; a challenge faced by even the largest retail companies.

Because M&M Meat Shops is built from hundreds of individual shops across Canada, each store approximately 1,500 square feet in size and doing approx-imately CDN$1 million a year in sales volume, smaller retailers can benefit from studying the activities at an individual store level. How the M&M Meat

Shops store owner works to identify 90% or more of their total sales and how they are able to make use of the information provided them in the form of regular management reports built around customer metrics are just some of the lessons applicable to smaller retailers.

M&M Meat Shops offers an invaluable case study for larger, multi-store retail companies. While customer information is beneficial at a headquarters level, assisting in the merchandising and marketing areas, the true power of customer data comes alive at the store level, where company associates interact with customers. M&M Meat Shops has not had the luxury of a corporate environment where orders can be issued from the head office; rather, M&M Meat Shops has had to create buy-in and understanding from each level of their organization in order to successfully gather and use customer data.

And of course M&M Meat Shops provides a model for other franchise companies wishing to develop customer literacy. From gathering tremendous levels of customer data to developing the infrastructure necessary to support not only collecting this data but also sending it back to store level where it can be most effectively used, M&M Meat Shops provides a world-class study. This model is also appropriate for wholesalers or distributors interested in developing similar structures for their retail customer stores.

Rice Epicurean Markets, based in Houston, Texas, has been at the leading edge of food retailing trends for some decades. One of the first to develop gourmet and specialty foods as the mainstay of their business, Rice Epicurean has also become a leading practitioner of understanding and using customer-based information to run their business.

Green Hills is a single, independent high-volume supermarket located in Syracuse, New York. Green Hills has been at the forefront of many of the developments related to the gathering and use of detailed customer information during much of the past decade. In my alternate life as CEO of Green Hills, I am privileged to have a retail environment in which to test new technologies, experiment with new marketing initiatives and work to integrate customer information into operations. We will encounter Green Hills in several areas throughout the book where we can draw upon the store's experiences to highlight certain concepts.

While I have sought to keep tables and reports to a minimum, such information is necessary for an understanding of the concepts presented. Further, the reports included here are actionable; they are samples of reporting used by active retailers to measure and manage their businesses. My advice: use these reports as tools, helping to create a structure within which you can unleash your operational and marketing creativity. Great possibilities await retailers able to think beyond one-dimensional product marketing, and even customer marketing; they are no longer mutually exclusive strategies. Such reporting tools provide a window into the interaction between your products and your customers.

I am very fortunate to be able to savor two careers simultaneously; I spend a portion of my time as a retail merchant, the balance as a consultant, assisting the retail industry with understanding the power of customer information. Such a combination allows me a unique perspective, conversant in the theory and concepts of using customer data, and able to put such theory into practice in a live retail environment.

It is a challenge to attempt to portray a multi-dimensional world in a two-dimensional medium: paper and ink. I am hopeful that through a combination of words, analogies, diagrams, and reports, the reader will be able to grasp the power of such knowledge.

RETAIL TODAY

Green Hills had its beginning as a small summer farm-stand opened in 1934. Located on the main thoroughfare heading south from the city of Syracuse, in the central part of New York State, the stand soon developed a loyal following. People headed to their camps on the lakes south of the city would stop to purchase their fresh vegetables, many times receiving them fresh from my great-grandmother Carrie's garden.

During the next 25 years, the stand grew bit by bit, adding some canned groceries, bread and other foodstuffs, until by the early 1960s it was a full-fledged supermarket. Green Hills was the quintessential small grocer, knowing most customers by name, their likes and dislikes, favorite products, and so on. But as the store grew, the emphasis became increasingly focused on products. And as the store grew into a sizeable business, the financial statements became the measurement tool for gauging success.

Sales were tallied each day using reports from the mechanical cash registers. Even these early machines were able to categorize sales by the primary product departments. The profit and loss statements mirrored the organization of the operation; structured along product-defined departments and categories. Gross profit margins were measured by departments, and then combined for a company total. Direct labor costs and supply expenses attributed back to each department so as to view the yield of each of the product-defined operational areas.

Retail is defined as the sale of goods in small quantities to the ultimate consumer. We can expand on this meaning of retail to include the two primary functions of a retail company: the procurement and distribution of goods, and the marketing and selling of those goods. As Green Hills grew quickly during the 1960s and early 70s, more and more management activities came to be focused upon the procurement of goods. Marketing, as was and still is prevalent in supermarket retailing, was largely centered on advertising circulars filled with products at special low prices.

Increasing amounts of trade monies began flowing from the manufacturers to the company to fund placement of the manufacturers' branded products in the ad circulars, to gain favorable shelf space and placement, and to support special deal prices to the consumer. It is without question that trade monies have heavily influenced the way many retail sectors have developed. An argument can be made that retail has developed the way it has, with a heavy bias towards managing products rather than customers, due to the trade monies used by the consumer packaged goods manufacturers in promoting their branded products. Retailers soon realized that product procurement could in itself become a profit center, a profit center without those sometimes bothersome customers.

While having dinner one evening with Jim Bright, President of Dunk and Bright Furniture, New York State's largest furniture store, I learned that such practices also exist in the furniture business. Jim explained to me that many furniture stores receive additional funds from the furniture manufacturers to feature their product lines in advertising, or to receive prime placement on the showroom floor.

Jim went on to explain that his company had also fallen into this trap, featuring certain manufacturers' lines so as to receive the additional funds, but not taking into regard the impact of this action on their customer base. Dunk and Bright found that the lines they were featuring were not necessarily the correct products to use if wanting to entice their targeted demographic consumer to visit the store. They have since found it far more profitable to become customer focused rather than product driven, passing up some trade monies in order to focus on the products that were more appealing to the customers Dunk and Bright desired.

We see this conundrum in a multitude of retail channels. Retailers that, while they say they are customer-focused, truly spend great resources working the supply end of their business for additional or incremental funding. Look at the next supermarket ad flyer you receive in your newspaper. The items on the front page are not placed there because the company knows that those are the products that most appeal to its most valuable customers. Many times those products are featured on the front page because the manufacturers have paid the retailer for that prime placement. Take notice of the end-cap, or end-of-aisle displays the next time you visit a supermarket; same thing. The products have been given the choicest real estate because it was paid for, little consumer focus involved.

It has become a commonplace practice for manufacturers to pay slotting fees so as to encourage distributors or retailers to carry new products. All this has created an environment such that many retailers simply see themselves as an extension of the distribution supply chain, the "last mile" connection to the end consumer. Many of these companies make a significant portion of their profits from such back-end monies, giving short shrift to satisfying their customers.

The sums spent on such trade monies are staggering. Typically, the consumer packaged goods companies do not release such figures, but an accounting rule change in 2001 forced many manufacturers to restate their revenues, deducting such payments, thus allowing observers to ascertain the magnitude of the monies involved. In 2001 alone, Kraft paid out over $4 billion in trade monies, a sum equal to 14% of their total revenues. Kellogg spent over $1 billion on such promotions, Coca-Cola over $2.5 billion, and Pepsi over $3 billion. All told, consumer packaged goods companies in the food industry spend over $60 billion a year on such trade promotions. [1]

Reinforcing this product focus, some manufacturers allocate their marketing support funds to retailers based upon the retailers' share of market. The share of market measurement itself is based upon product sales. By linking trade monies to share of market measures, the consumer packaged goods companies have created a self-sustaining cycle; retailers concentrating on moving cases of product to sustain and grow their share of market measures to maximize their trade monies, which are linked to the share of market measure. Retailers have every incentive, from internal benchmarking to external measures, to continuously grow their product sales. Where in this system is the individual consumer?

As such trade monies have increasingly gushed forth over the past several decades, retailers have, in many cases, come to rely on such monies to support their margins and profitability. It has created strong incentives for retailers to concentrate on simply moving cases of product, usually via price promotion, to increase their share of such monies. In part, this practice has lulled many retailers into a stupor; they have been able to sustain their businesses through basic item and price advertising. Many retailers have become distributors, not merchants actively marketing their stores and products.

Returning to Green Hills, as product scanning systems entered the store the quantity and quality of information available began to quickly improve. Products were scanned upon delivery at the receiving area, and scanned again going out through the POS system. Green Hills was now able to more accurately measure product movement and sales, thus laying the foundation for product category management initiatives.

Food retailers have been at the forefront of the development of product category management. Products are segmented into categories, such as cereal or fresh juice, and a category manager appointed. This category manager is responsible for the sales and margin produced by his or her category. They negotiate with the suppliers for deals, trade monies, and so on, in addition to planning advertising and marketing.

This practice has become a tool for extracting even more funds from the manufacturers. It has become common practice for the retailer to appoint one of the leading suppliers in a given category as the "category captain". Of course, the supplier must pay for such a privilege. In addition, the retailer hopes to capitalize on the manufacturer's greater marketing skills and access to market-wide product movement information to help plan space allocation and price points within the category.

Borders, the book and music retailer, has recently announced to publishers that it is embarking on a similar strategy. [2] Ostensibly, Borders hopes to draw on the publishers' access to additional information to assist with decision making regarding which books to carry in certain categories, pricing, and so on. The retailer is also looking for the publishers to help fund market research and other work to benefit Borders. Similar practices are taking root in the convenience store, drug chain, and mass merchants channels.

As things progressed at Green Hills, sales and margins became the basis for management incentives, thus ingraining into the culture the importance of these product-based measures. Management was now rewarded from product-based measures, leading at times to decision making more in line with maximizing those sales and margin measures, not necessarily what was best for customers. Product-based measures became ever-more accurate, and more pervasive. Slowly but surely, products began taking center stage in terms of management time.

As scanning systems and rates improved, facilitated by technology and improved communications between supplier and retailer, the stage was set for further gains on the part of the retail industry. This improved information led to industry-wide initiatives: activity based costing, efficient consumer response, scan-based trading, and so on. The goal of each of these initiatives has been the same: improved product logistics, lowering the cost of moving items from point of manufacture to the retail sales shelf and out the door.

Over the past five or six decades, similar scenarios have played out in the major retail channels; from supermarkets to drug stores, discount stores to department stores, product-based business measures have ruled the day. As business people, we could only manage that which we could measure: products.

One of the difficulties of focusing on supply chain logistics is that successful practices tend to be quickly replicated by others, thus negating their long-term competitive advantage. Wal-Mart's success in developing product logistics as a tour de force lies more in their focus and discipline than in magical revolutions in how products are handled. The majority of retailers tend to give such efforts the once-over rather than intensive study and progress.

It can be argued that it is this myopic focus on products, at the expense of customers, that has brought many retail channels to their present predicament. Many retail sectors today are mature, experiencing low, if any, organic growth. Compounding the problem is the fact that many areas are over-stored, the pace of retail space growth outdistancing population growth. According to research done by F.W. Dodge, the retail industry added 3 square feet of new store space for every man, woman and child in the U.S. during the 1990s. That rate of growth was approximately double the population growth during that same decade. [3]

As organic growth has slowed in many sectors, retail companies see acquisition and consolidation as the only growth opportunity remaining. And as a handful of companies reach a dominant market share position in their home countries, they are looking outside, becoming global in their scope and reach. By one recent study, 23 of the largest 25 retailers have operations spread around the world. [4]

Some suggest that the growth of Wal-Mart has triggered this trend towards consolidation; retail companies looking to bulk up, developing the purchasing power and efficiencies of scale so as to compete with the world's largest retailer. Others state that the trend towards fewer, larger companies is a natural result of competition spreading across traditional retail channels. Yet others suggest that growth by acquisition is a natural state of a maturing retail industry in which organic growth slows. While the cause and effect can be endlessly debated, the end result is the same: consolidation is occurring in many mass retail channels in a multitude of markets around the world.

From figures assembled by the Food Marketing Institute, in the year 2000 the top five U.S. supermarket retailers held a combined 40% market share; six short years prior the same share was held by the top 20 companies. [5] In Australia, the three largest food retailers account for 80% of the total market. In Canada, the top 10 retail food companies account for 80% of all grocery sales [6]; the top three, Loblaws, Sobeys, and Safeway, account for 50% alone. In France, the top five food retailers control a 90% market share; in Germany 60% of the market share is held by the five largest companies. [7]

The retail food industry is not the only channel experiencing such tremendous consolidation. In the U.S., the consumer electronics channel is now largely dominated by two companies, Best Buy and Circuit City [8]; not long ago there were a number of active electronics retailers. The drug store channel is yet another example; within the past few years we have seen CVS acquiring Revco and Arbor Drug, Rite Aid taking over Thrifty/Payless and JCPenney combining its Thrift Drug company with Eckerd. The number of drug store companies in the U.S. declined 28% from 1990 to 1998. [9]

Remember just a few years ago the number of computer retailers in the market? Today just one, CompUSA, is the sole survivor. The department store channel offers much the same story: Federated acquiring Macy's; Proffitt's, itself an amalgamation of smaller department stores, taking over Saks Fifth Avenue.

The convenience store sector has seen a number of mergers and acquisitions between major oil companies, the largest refiners looking to build greater market share so as to control more of their supply channel. Further, convenience store operators themselves are either purchasing other companies or are in turn being purchased. Couche-Tard, Canada's largest convenience store operator, has been aggressively acquiring U.S.-based convenience stores, making it the ninth-largest convenience store operator in the U.S. Couche-Tard now operates over 2,000 stores between Canada and the United States.

Consolidation is happening everywhere. Wal-Mart's acquisition of ASDA has shaken the U.K. marketplace; in fourth place when purchased, ASDA is now closing in on the number two position as measured by market share. Wal-Mart is providing a taste of its discount operation to the people of Germany through its acquisition of Wertkauf, a hypermarket operator. Carrefour has absorbed Promodes to create the world's second-largest retail company with operations spanning the globe.

The tsunami of consolidation is now beginning to strike the shores of Asia. The poor economic climate of Japan is providing fertile conditions for massive consolidation to occur as global retailers Wal-Mart and Tesco enter the market, adding to the existing pressures created by the presence of Costco and Carrefour. Already the signs of the coming shakeout in the Japanese retail scene are evident.

In industry after industry, these retail behemoths are exerting more and more pressure upon smaller retailers, threatening their very survival. The large companies are able to use their purchasing power for improved terms from suppliers and manufacturers; combined with development of superior logistics systems, creating intense profit margin pressures for other retailers trying to keep pace. Leveraging their size also allows these retail giants to negotiate better lease arrangements and improved terms with other suppliers, providing more tertiary advantages that their smaller competitors cannot match.

Closely related to the trend of consolidation is the trend of channel blurring. In some cases it appears that this blurring of traditional retail lines has been one of the causes of consolidation.

The continued growth of Wal-Mart is again frequently mentioned as a leading cause of channel blurring. The development of the Wal-Mart Supercenter, combining a full supermarket with a traditional Wal-Mart discount operation, seems to have kicked-off a movement amongst many retailers to combine food with other offerings. While similar retail concepts, such as hypermarkets, have succeeded in Europe for years, and even similar companies such as Meijer have been successful in the U.S., none of these have had the momentum of Wal-Mart to create shock waves throughout the retailing industry.

Increasingly, everyone is selling everything. From large discounters, to convenience stores, to even office supply retailers, food has become a way for retailers in other channels to foster frequency of shopping visits. By offering staple items such as milk and bread at very low prices, non-food retailers are able to entice shoppers to their stores on a more frequent basis, in turn making other purchases that are profitable to the retailer while there.

In response, we see the traditional food retailers bringing other lines of merchandise into their stores to bolster sales and margins. Giant Stores, a division of Ahold, has been developing a store-within-a-store concept with Toys "R" Us, essentially locating a condensed toy store in the middle of the supermarket. Tops Friendly Markets, another U.S. based division of Ahold, is following a similar plan. K-B Toys is providing merchandise to stock toy sections in over 1,000 Safeway stores.[10] Loblaws of Canada recently announced that they would begin selling self-assembly furniture, a.k.a. Ikea. Walgreens, one of the premier U.S. drug store chains, has been experimenting with fresh produce in some stores.

This trend of channel blurring is creating some surprising combinations. Office Depot announced they will open shops inside Stop & Shop Supermarkets, selling office products. Is this a supermarket selling office supplies or an office supply store selling food? And in a "reverse channel blur" move driven by a product manufacturer, Proctor and Gamble, looking for new ways to boost sales of mainstay brands, is looking outside traditional channels, recently announcing they would begin selling Tide detergent in Home Depot stores.

The convenience store channel provides an excellent case study; convenience store operators are increasingly at risk of channel blurring. At an accelerating pace, supermarkets are installing fueling centers in their parking lots. By tying gasoline purchases together with the customer's food purchases through their loyalty marketing programs, these traditional supermarket operators have claimed a sizeable stake of all gasoline sales within the U.S. very quickly, and their share is growing. To make matters worse, Wal-Mart currently operates about 400 fuel centers in the U.S. and is planning another 100 in Canada, creating yet more pressure on this beleaguered channel. In a further swipe at the convenience store industry, Jack in the Box, the United States' fourth-largest hamburger chain, has announced it will convert a quarter of its nearly 2,000 outlets to a combination gasoline-convenience store-restaurant format over the next few years. [11]

A recent study by Energy Analysts International projects that these interlopers will attain a 16% share of total fuel sales by 2005; a large enough share to put a number of convenience store operators at risk.

As retail competition continues to intensify, retailers in all channels are looking for non-traditional product offerings that may provide them an edge. One can ponder the strategic vision behind this channel blurring movement. While such combinations may be made for tactical reasons, the long term strategy is open to debate. In the eyes of the consumer, what is the difference between a Giant supermarket with a toy section and a Safeway with a toy section down the street? And does Stop & Shop not risk their identity as a food retailer when bringing together office supplies and toys under its store banner? Stop & Shop stores more and more resembling supercenters; supercenters in turn increasingly resembling the large supermarkets bringing in countless other product lines. Does uniqueness no longer count when a business exceeds a certain size?

Studies have shown that consumers are shunning brand loyalty, instead making their purchasing decisions based upon price. To a large degree, consumers perceive many branded products as commodities, not enough differences between competing brands to justify a substantial price differential. One can, in addition, make the argument that this view extends to retailers themselves; consumers in many cases not experiencing any substantial difference between competing retailers, thus again leading to price-based decision making and further exacerbating the product-based retail challenge.

Unless a retail company can lay claim, both in actuality and in the consumer's mind, to a very clear product-based position, they run the risk of becoming commoditized. Setting aside the location factor for a moment (and location is becoming less of a factor given home delivery and internet purchasing), we can view these positions as shown in Figure 1-1. Often we see retailers taking a strong position on one factor, and assuming a position on par with competitors relative to other factors.

This concept is well-presented by Fred Crawford and Ryan Mathews in their book The Myth of Excellence. [12] Throughout the book the authors build a strong case encouraging companies to focus on one area to excel in, essentially staking out that factor as their territory in the marketplace and in the mind of the consumer, while maintaining some level of parity with competitors in other areas. Crawford and Mathews suggest that companies trying to be the "best" in all operational areas typically do not meet industry benchmarks in any.

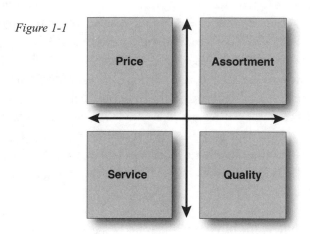

Figure 1-1

Traditional Dimensions of Product-Based Retail Strategy

There is characteristically room in a given market for a retailer to successfully occupy a market position predicated upon one of the four product-based factors. In other words, a retailer can stake out a competitive position by being perceived as having the lowest price, or having the greatest product assortment, or offering the highest quality, or the greatest customer service. In practice, these four attributes do not operate independently;

many times there are strong correlations between price and quality or price and service.

Aldi, the German-based food retailer, provides an excellent example of a company owning a clear-cut market position. With approximately 500 stores in the U.S., Aldi stores are very low cost, no frills, warehouse-type stores offering private label or secondary packer label foodstuffs. Product is often sold right out of the case in which it was shipped, and the limited meat and produce is packaged. The stores are minimally staffed — customers must bag their own groceries — and the shopping carts require a twenty-five cent deposit, which is returned to the customer upon returning the trolley. Aldi maintains a near-religious focus on controlling costs so as to offer the lowest retail prices. Aldi owns a very clear product-based position in the market.

Neiman Marcus provides an example from the other end of the spectrum, perhaps the most upscale department store in the United States. Through economic boom times to downturns, Neiman Marcus has never wavered in its focus on haute couture and designer clothing collections. By doing so it has steadfastly maintained its position in the industry, and in the mind of its customer.

Losing a clear-cut market position can rapidly marginalize a retailer. Consider Food Lion, the U.S. division of Delhaize, the Belgian food retailer. For a number of years, during the 1970s and 80s, Food Lion was the epitome of an everyday low price retailer. Similar to Aldi, the stores offered no frills, and were obsessed with controlling costs. As the company continued to grow during the 1990s with increased competition, Food Lion began to lose focus, feeling it, too, must offer in-store bakery departments and delicatessens. It did not take long for Food Lion to muddle its image in the marketplace, appearing as a rather poor stepchild to the more established supermarkets. Food Lion had forsaken the market position that had built their company.

Notice how the examples cited tend to be from opposite ends of the same price-based continuum; retailers either owning a very clear position as low price or owning the position of offering the most upscale and expensive offerings. Retailers, perhaps starting more towards one extreme or the other of the price continuum, have a strong tendency to migrate towards the middle as a result of competition or greed, à la Food Lion. A multitude of retail channels are filled with examples of such companies, having marginalized their businesses due to commoditization.

When combined with the trend of channel blurring, this commoditization creates a frightening picture for retailers of any size. When the same products, or very similar products, are offered everywhere, why not buy at the lowest price? One has to look no further than the supermarket ad flyers in the newspaper to see this concept in action; all competitors offer the same items — lowest price wins. As leading clothing brands, such as Polo Ralph Lauren and Nautica, have created store-within-a-store concepts at competing department stores, there is virtually no difference between the department stores themselves; each is selling the same products, many times from identical displays.

This commoditization leads us to a discussion of brand marketing. It is very challenging to build a strong brand image and impression when the product is being price-promoted by every retailer in the market. It is the same dilemma that is creating yet more pressures for the retailers competing with Tier One companies in many retail channels. As consolidation and channel blurring have served to focus more competition on price, with the same branded goods available in a number of places, some retailers are heading off in new directions. There exists a diverging movement with regard to marketing and the role of branded goods and commodities.

The largest retail companies are realizing the need for unique product offerings so as to differentiate themselves from their competitors; they understand the forces of commoditization and the need to create new strategies. These companies are of the size that they can create their own controlled label products, unique to their stores; and we are seeing the leaders in every major channel pursuing such a strategy.

Loblaws of Canada was one of the early leaders in perceiving the advantages of a strong private-label offering, developing one of the premier programs in food retailing with their President's Choice (PC) line of goods. In contrast to the traditional food retailer's view of prioritizing price and margin first, quality second, Loblaws committed to putting forth top quality products. In many cases, they took aim at the national brand leader in each category; Loblaws developed a superior product at a comparable price point that still offered a strong margin opportunity.

So strong was this effort that Loblaws budgeted over CDN$10 million annually to support product development. After successfully developing PC counterparts to the leading national brands in the largest categories, such as cookies and soft drink, Loblaws next turned its attention to developing unique items that, while not offering tremendous sales volumes, helped to create a halo effect for the brand and the stores. A notable example is provided by the "Memories of..." sauces, famous within the President's Choice line. Created by Dave Nichol of Loblaws, the PC "Memories of…" sauces were developed to capitalize on his culinary travels about the globe. An impressive dinner one evening in Kobe, Japan, for example, culminated in the Memories of Kobe sauce so Nichol could share the flavors of his exotic meal with his Canadian customers.

Other companies are looking to align themselves with niche retailers that already enjoy strong brand recognition. Ahold's Stop & Shop division recently crafted a deal by which Dunkin' Donuts will operate shops within the large Stop & Shop supermarkets. Dunkin' Donuts is further capitalizing on this trend by announcing a test of a store-within-a-store concept with Home Depot. A similar strategy is at work in the purchase by Sears of the popular Lands' End catalog merchant. Lands' End enjoys a very strong brand relationship with its customers; Sears will be looking to capitalize on that strength by offering Lands' End products in its stores. Starbucks has announced they will open shops in new and remodeled Target stores. And Circuit City will begin offering products from The Sharper Image through dedicated kiosks in their stores. [13]

Looking at the discount channel we see similar strategies appearing. While Kmart was unsuccessful in many areas of its operation, one of its bright spots was the licensing of the Martha Stewart line of goods and making the line exclusive to Kmart. Even as the company winds its way through bankruptcy, the Martha Stewart line is seen as one of its strongest assets that the company hopes to retain. Kmart also has exclusive rights within the discount channel to products licensed from Disney and Sesame Street.

Toys "R" Us, under siege in the toy category from Wal-Mart, is narrowing its product offerings, and working towards developing more exclusive offerings that consumers cannot find elsewhere. Target is the exclusive retailer for products designed by Michael Graves, Mossimo Giannulli, Todd Oldham and other designers [14], enabling Target to be viewed as the discounter with style. Wal-Mart also understands the value of exclusive offerings, recently announcing it would import the George line of apparel from its U.K. based ASDA subsidiary to the U.S. market.

Within the past decade, several of the leading fashion houses have gone public, companies such as Polo Ralph Lauren, Jones Apparel Group and Tommy Hilfiger. These companies, now under pressure from Wall Street, can no longer ignore the thriving discount sector, while their traditional department store outlets are stagnating. A number of these fashion houses are creating alternate, related brands to offer through discounters such as Kohl's. The effect: further pressure on the department stores that no longer have exclusivity on in-demand fashion labels. Federated Department Stores is responding to this situation by pushing hard to establish its I.N.C. in-house fashion brand, positioning it as a trendy fashion brand exclusive to Federated stores.

While such product strategies are proper for the largest retailers that can fund such efforts, the effect of these programs is yet further pressure being exerted on smaller retail competitors. The largest retailers are able to use the generous profit margins supplied by their private label products to fund even lower retail prices on commodity items to lure consumers into their stores. This simply reinforces the commodity pricing spiral impacting on so many smaller and mid-size retail companies in a multitude of channels.

In the early 1990s, Loblaws created a merchandising intelligence system called Merlin. Using the transaction-level data gained through its scanning point of sale systems, Loblaws executives could monitor and analyze any given product category, seeing at a glance the movement, sales, and margins of both the national brands and their private label offerings. Through such information, Loblaws developed the strategy of product "shielding"; they would under-price their competitors on key national brand items but merchandise in-store on either side of the national brand their private label products at an even lower price, providing strong inducement for the consumer to purchase the private label product rather than the national brand that brought them into the store. Through such strategies, Loblaws was able to consistently deliver stronger margins than its competitors while going to market with more aggressive pricing on key brands.

For the retailers not able to fund development and marketing of strong private label programs, they find themselves being forced to go to market using brand name products; competing not only against the giants but against their other competitors in the same position, each going to market with the same products. Such an environment breeds the commoditizing of brand name goods; he who has the lowest price wins. This impact is being felt by the manufacturers of these products in addition to the retailers.

John Mahar, Director of Operations for Green Hills, offers a perceptive take on the predicament in which many of today's consumer packaged goods manufacturers find themselves. Mahar's view is that once a branded product is offered on Wal-Mart's store shelves it has become a commodity. The reasoning is straightforward: Wal-Mart is able to sell such goods at everyday low prices due to its prowess in logistics and purchasing clout. Other retailers, having to compete but unable to match the everyday low price, will price promote the product, many times requesting assistance in funding price promotions from the manufacturer. At this point, the manufacturer has lost all control over a suggested retail price, thus losing control of perceived brand equity.

Rather than building brand equity, such situations result in many products being viewed by consumers as always on sale. These branded goods become nothing more than another commodity; sold as products regularly available on "deal", the true value not the suggested retail price, but the sale price.

Companies basing their business upon a unique product offering may have had some successes in the past, but it is becoming increasingly difficult to maintain a clear market position over time solely based on product attributes. It does not take long before others come to market with offerings similar to the unique products, thus marginalizing and commoditizing yet another retail competitive factor. At times, this damage is done by companies themselves, believing that a successful brand can be extended.

Levi Strauss & Co. has embarked on a decidedly rocky road in the branding world. From a peak of over $7 billion in sales in 1996, Levi's sales had fallen to slightly over $4 billion by 2001. Desperate to regain its financial perform-ance, Levi has turned to the mass discount channel in an attempt to revive its fortunes. Creating a line extension called Levi Strauss Signature, Levi Strauss has announced the new line will be available in Wal-Mart stores and sell for less than $30. At the same time, Levi is trying to capture the designer part of the market with Levi Strauss Vintage, attempting to sell the jeans through high-end retailers like Neiman Marcus and Barneys New York. [15] Time will tell, but it is hard to accept that high-end consumers will be willing to pay premium prices for a product bearing such close resemblance (in form, function, and name) to one sold in Wal-Mart. While such line extensions sometimes work in the consumer packaged goods industry, it may be a difficult sell in the fashion industry. Truly successful brands do not try to be everything to everybody.

So we see that retail companies are being forced to think beyond the one-dimensional world of products and pricing in order to compete in the marketplace. For an increasing number of companies, attempting to develop themselves as a brand in the mind of the consumer offers the hope of moving beyond pure product-based competition. Such companies are very aware that building a brand in retail equates to the shopping experience itself. Looking about in most any retail sector, those companies most successful are often characterized by possessing a strong brand image, the retailer aware that the shopping experience they provide their clientele is the result of a multitude of small factors all done well. From the moment a consumer enters a store's parking lot or, for those in malls or plazas, the proximity of the store entrance, the shopping experience begins.

The customer's shopping experience is continued and influenced by everything he or she sees, feels, touches, smells, and hears; at times these interactions are conscious, at other times they register on the subconscious — but they are all important. From the appearance of the staff, to the tone of voice used by the cashier, to the smell of freshly brewed coffee, to the visual appeal of a display, retailers need to be cognizant that all such factors impact upon their "brand". All of these factors must now be managed, in addition to the basics of well-stocked shelves, clean floors, competitive pricing, proper assortment, and a modicum of customer service. For retailers enlightened to the concept of viewing the retail shopping experience as integral to brand building, the challenges can appear overwhelming.

Traditionally, the concept of branding has, of course, applied to products themselves. Consumer packaged goods companies have been adept at creating an impression that forms within the consumer's mind when hearing a certain product's name or seeing the product image. Many times the image and emotional connotation formed have nothing directly to do with the product or use of the product itself. Like the television commercial showing the mother congratulating her son after a winning soccer game, and then linking this image to a laundry detergent, a great deal of branding relies on creating an emotional tug or connection, filling the consumer with the appropriate thoughts associated with a specific product. By purchasing that particular brand of laundry detergent, the consumer envisions herself (or himself) enjoying that moment of bonding with her child.

When we objectively consider the distance between the manufacturer of a product and the ultimate consumer, the consumer packaged goods industry has done an impressive job in developing a connection between millions of consumers and their product brand. Certainly this connection will only go so far; all other things being equal, the manufacturer hopes that it is enough to cause the consumer to choose their brand when in the store, confronted by a dizzying array of similar products.

Stop for a moment and consider the power of branding when applied to a retail company itself. A retailer is close to the consumer, the retailer's staff directly interacting with the customer on a personal, one-to-one level. The retailer controls the store environment in which the consumer shops, able to alter any and all factors so as to build a brand image with the customer based upon their actual shopping experience; not an image built upon experience-by-association as done through television commercials.

It has been the manufacturing industry, specifically consumer packaged goods companies, that have developed many of the skills and knowledge necessary for creating the marketing messages upon which good branding is built. The consumer packaged goods companies have had to develop these skills in order to sell their products, as they do not directly control the "final mile" of the supply chain that directly interacts with the consumer. Additionally, the greater profit margins inherent in manufacturing help provide the necessary funds to support such endeavors and skill sets within the organization.

Retailers, on the other hand, are often constrained by relatively low profit margins, rendering many retailers unable to afford high-priced marketing staff.

For decades, mass retailers could go to market advertising goods and products made by others, at times supported by advertising funds from the manufacturer. For many retail companies, the concept of branding and marketing has meant maximizing the number of branded products they can pack into ad flyers. The notion of branding, having to think through all the minute interactions a customer can have while shopping within a store, is almost too much for traditional retailers; it's easier to just lower the price for the next ad circular distribution and hope that it attracts more consumers to the door.

As an enlightening exercise, imagine for a moment that you no longer have the ability to use price promotion of products in your store, marketing or advertising. You must go to market without these tools which most retailers have come to take for granted. Such thoughts are usually enough to give retailers nightmares. But now think of how you can attract customers to your stores, how you are going to retain customers, get them to come back after visiting your store for the first time. Such an exercise begins to quickly drive home the importance of all those heretofore inconsequential factors so easily overlooked on a daily basis. What does the area around the store entrance look like; is it inviting? What is the first impression a customer has upon entering the store? What are the sounds, sights, smells?

The customer's shopping experience is the new retail battleground; good locations, the right product assortment, competitive pricing, and all the other attributes of good retailing are the price of entry. But if we go even further and link strong branding skills and operations with customer information, we are creating a retail tour de force. Such retail companies can now use their customer intelligence to further reinforce their brand experience, particularly to those customers who meet the retailer's criteria as a valuable or potentially valuable client. In many cases, retailers today must think far beyond simply putting a product on the shelf. Leaders understand that they must consider how the shopping experience is impacted upon even after the customer has left with their purchases.

Nordstrom has won acclaim for its customer service for many years, realizing the value in providing exceptional service to customers and burnishing their brand. While shopping in a Nordstrom store I came across a jacket I wished to purchase for an upcoming trip but the store did not have the correct size. Tom G., the salesperson assisting me, told me he would pick the jacket up from another store the next day and overnight it to me. While paying for my purchases, I remarked about the legendary Nordstrom service; another customer overhearing me related a recent story of a Nordstrom salesperson delivering a robe, pajamas, and slippers to her husband in the hospital as her husband had been admitted on an emergency basis during the day and did not have any provisions with him.

Imagine the power of combining this level of service with detailed customer information on a majority of Nordstrom's customers. Nordstrom has signaled its intent to move in this direction by partnering with Blue Martini Software. Utilizing Blue Martini's software expertise, Nordstrom will help their sales representatives track customer purchases, storing individual customers' information in a central database accessible by the associate through the POS system.

Retail companies possessing customer data are able to continue their relationship with the customer beyond the transaction; able to communicate with the consumer at other touch-points in the store, such as at kiosks or the POS, or at home using e-mail, telephone, or even direct mail. Such capabilities make the idea of extending the shopping experience beyond the store's walls a much more realistic endeavor. Each of these communications, or customer "touches", must be used to build and reinforce the retailer's brand; the shopping experience.

Over the years there have been numerous initiatives and concepts put forth as the strategy du jour, from category management to activity based costing, from efficient consumer response to supply chain management. As various retail sectors have evolved and matured, activities that are perceived as business strategies are in reality manifestations of a maturing product-based business model. Years ago product-driven initiatives such as the development of private label or different store formats allowed the retailer to capture substantially improved margins for some period of time. As competition has grown faster and fiercer, it is increasingly hard to create advantage that is lasting.

These market forces create pressure for retailers to seek a new competitive position; many feel that loyalty marketing or customer relationship management initiatives offer that potential. Thinking that if they can learn who their customers are, and what they're buying, the retailer seeks to sell their customers more and improve retention of customers over time. I addressed the idea of this polarization occurring in retail; companies shifting from a non-competitive product-based position to a customer-based strategy in my book, Building the Customer Specific Retail Enterprise. At the time this was an accurate scenario and description of what was occurring in the marketplace, but in hindsight it didn't go far enough. The retail winners of tomorrow realize that to fully maximize their business potential, they must completely understand both their product logistics and their customer logistics; they must master the multiple dimensions of retail.

Loyalty marketing programs in retail continue to be most prevalent in the supermarket channel throughout the world, but the picture is changing rapidly. More and more we are seeing such programs appearing in other channels, notably chain drug stores, hypermarkets, discounters, and department stores. The list goes on to include specialty and niche retailers, bookstores; even Starbucks is laying the foundation for a customer knowledge program through its prepayment card. More and more retail companies in a multitude of sectors are developing a continuous flow of customer data through their enterprises.

The companies realizing the greatest success from developing customer knowledge view it as a long term business strategy, not a marketing promotion designed to provide a short term boost to sales. These companies understand that detailed customer information, properly structured, provides new ways to measure retail business performance and create new dimensions in marketing opportunities. These are the companies that are driven from the highest levels of management to obtain high levels of information gathering, and to base business strategies on an understanding of customer information.

THE CASE FOR CUSTOMER DATA

The collection of customer data in retailing first gained momentum during the late 1980s with the launch of Citicorp's Reward America program. Designed as an electronic latter day version "S&H Green Stamp" program, Citi's goal was to capture large amounts of consumer identified, transaction level data, which would be collected and then resold to consumer packaged goods companies. Due to a host of factors, not the least of which was the high cost of massive computing power, this pioneering effort at gathering and using detailed customer information soon failed.

Though the Reward America program did not succeed, enough appetites had been whetted that with the advent of personal computers and decreased computing costs, forward-thinking retailers envisioned capturing and using customer data themselves. Ukrops, a Richmond, Virginia, based supermarket retailer and one of the early Reward America participants, realized there was no turning back after seeing data on their own customers' shopping behavior. They and a small number of other pioneer retailers in the early 1990s, many in the supermarket channel, assembled their own initiatives to begin collecting detailed customer information.

Through the 1990s frequent shopper programs exploded through the supermarket channel, most aggressively in the U.S. and Europe, eventually throughout Asia. The recent past has seen these efforts spreading to other retail sectors throughout the world.

Specifically, what customer information is captured through these efforts? In the typical frequent shopper program, customers are encouraged to join the retailer's "club" by completing an application asking for name and contact information. In return, the customer is provided a frequent shopper card or key tag which they are encouraged to use each time they shop to receive certain benefits or privileges. Essentially the bar coded (or magnetic-striped) card provides a way to scan the customer when they check out, appending the customer's identification number to the transaction. The transactions are then compiled into large databases, providing retailers a view of customers' shopping behavior over time.

Two primary incentive schemes quickly evolved to entice consumers to join such programs; in the U.S. markets the predominant program became price-based, tying the customer's frequent shopper card to the store's weekly specials; in Europe, points-based schemes became the prevalent form of loyalty programs, essentially offering the consumer a 1% rebate based upon their purchasing. As a select group of the early pioneers soon discovered, the wealth of such programs lay in the data collected, not necessarily the loyalty scheme itself.

As a key group of retailers about the world have found, a deep understanding of the power of customer information leads to a profound shift in how management of retail companies perceive their world. The transformation arising from the ability to view and measure customer behavior over time is akin to operating in a darkened store and bringing the surroundings into view by turning on the lights. Retailers are now able to move beyond the confinement provided by a transactional view of their customers to a much broader perspective.

Consider that for decades, since the advent of mass retailing, retailers have had to think in terms of transactions, the only view of customers possible. Yes, as retailers we "knew" that our regular customers would shop with us on a more frequent basis than other customers, but we couldn't measure this frequency. It was very cumbersome to reward customers for their shopping behavior over time. Customers were rewarded within the confines of a transaction, usually by means of special prices or discounts.

With the expanded horizon provided by detailed customer information, great differences in customer value came to light, and have been observed in most every retail channel.

Some time ago I attended a brainstorming session of some leading convenience store operators in the U.S. They had begun to understand the concepts of customer intelligence and were being influenced by many of the larger supermarket companies now offering gasoline, tying their offerings together through their loyalty platform. As we discussed the concepts involved, and began to move toward more specifics, the question of economics very quickly came to the fore. This same discussion also brought to light the danger implicit in dealing with averages when applied to customer information and customer behavior.

One participant advanced the argument that "the average consumer drives 12,000 miles per year, averaging 25 miles per gallon. This means that they are purchasing 480 gallons of gasoline, in total, each year. At an average cost of approximately $1.50 per gallon, with an average gross margin of 12%, this doesn't leave much money to reward loyalty!" People having studied customer shopping behavior understand that there is no such thing as an "average" customer. In the case of convenience stores, customers purchasing premium gas rather than the lowest grade available are paying more per gallon and the retailer is making a larger margin on the sale. And, as is often the case when discussing customer shopping behavior, we must look beyond the individual's purchasing to the purchasing behavior of the family or household; the multiplier effect.

Moving further, if the customer purchases merchandise inside the convenience store, such as milk or other consumables, the retailer is generating even higher levels of sales and greater margins. Convenience store customers are not all equal in economic value to the retailer, nor is there such a thing as an "average" customer. Report 2-1 presents actual customer data from a convenience store company offering gas.

Decile	Gas/Convenience Stores		
	Average Spend Per Year	Avg. # Transactions Per Year	Average Spend Per Transaction
10	$5,670.69	172.5	$32.87
9	$3,422.11	87.1	$39.29
8	$2,589.54	66.4	$39.00
7	$2,007.26	53.2	$37.73
6	$1,511.35	43.4	$34.82
5	$1,042.24	34.2	$30.47
4	$630.80	23.5	$26.84
3	$329.70	13.3	$24.79
2	$138.55	5.8	$23.89
1	$37.75	1.9	$19.87

* Data provided by Visible Results (www.visibleresults.com)

As is clear from Report 2-1, there are tremendous differences in customer shopping behavior in the convenience store sector; the highest spending customer spends over 150 times the amount of the lowest spending customer over the course of the year. We also see a strong correlation between spending and shopping frequency; the highest spending customers have over 170 transactions per year, the lowest spending customers only two. And, an additional trend we see across most retail channels, a corresponding variation in the average transaction amount; higher spending customers typically spend more in each transaction than lower spending consumers.

Any person who has spent time on a retail sales floor instinctively understands that there are great differences in shopping behavior amongst consumers. Some customers are seen on a regular basis, some infrequently; some customers have full shopping carts, others with just a product or two. But it was only with the advent of collecting customer data that retail companies could truly begin to understand and document customer shopping behavior. Retailers having customer level data can now see the customers behind the transactions. And what a different view it provides.

Customer value is dictated by the customer's shopping behavior relative to four factors; spending, shopping frequency, the profit margin of the products or services purchased, and the customer's shopping behavior over time.

Customer Value Derived From 4 Factors...

$ Average Spend per Visit
X   Frequency of Shopping
X   Gross Profit Margin of Products Purchase
X   Time
_____

= **Customer Value**

Customer value dictated by spending and shopping frequency is self-explanatory. Retailers often sell different products or services at different levels of profit margin throughout their stores; the mix a customer purchases then further contributes to the value of the customer to the company. A retailer's pricing strategy can further exacerbate differences in customer value related to the mix of products or services purchased; retailers going to market using a high-low marketing strategy further skew the range of values.

It has been well documented that retailers can have a substantial amount of churn occurring in their customer bases; some customers shopping once or twice never to be seen again, other customers remaining with the company for years. Obviously, the longer the time frame we are able to analyze, the greater the variation in customer value.

There exists a very strong correlation between spending and frequency, but attempting to learn which drives which is much like the proverbial chicken and egg question; in the end it really does not matter, it is simply enough to understand the connection. The nuances involved in increasing spending or shopping frequency is a marketing discussion; one we will hold until a later section.

The most widespread view of consumer value is based upon purchasing. Ranking a customer population by spending, and then dividing into equal size segments (for example, deciles) presents the variations in customer value quite clearly. For example, Report 2-2 is an example of customer data drawn from a supermarket retailer, reported on a per-store average.

Decile Report

Decile	# of Customers	# of Visits Over Year	Avg. Trans. per Week	Avg. $ per Visit	Decile Spending	% of Total	Cumulative %
10	2,671	83.7	1.61	$45.45	$10,161,647.00	59.4%	59.4%
9	2,671	42.1	0.81	$27.69	$3,113,702.00	18.2%	77.6%
8	2,671	24	0.46	$24.41	$1,564,890.00	9.1%	86.8%
7	2,671	14.7	0.28	$22.70	$891,308.00	5.2%	92.0%
6	2,671	9.6	0.18	$21.25	$544,806.00	3.4%	95.3%
5	2,671	6.3	0.12	$20.55	$345,851.00	2.0%	97.4%
4	2,671	4.4	0.08	$18.58	$218,307.00	1.3%	98.6%
3	2,671	3	0.06	$16.58	$132,857.00	0.8%	99.4%
2	2,671	2	0.04	$13.67	$73,003.00	0.4%	99.8%
1	2,671	1.3	0.03	$8.06	$27,984.00	0.2%	100.0%
Total	**26,710**	**19.1**	**0.37**	**$33.47**	**$17,074,355.00**	**100%**	

In the supermarket channel, with little variation, we see that the top 30% of customers (when ranked by spending) generate approximately 75-85% of the retailer's annual turnover (in this retailer's case the skewing is slightly more, the top 30% providing nearly 87% of total sales), the bottom 30% of customers providing less than 3% of annual sales. Such variances in customer value are evident around the world, no matter the size of the retailer or sector.

Such large differences in shopping behavior are also evident when looking at shopping frequency. Green Hills, an independent supermarket whose customer behavior is not atypical in the food retailing channel, has found that its best customers shop several times per week; consumers in the least valuable customer segment appear in the store on average only once every two to three months. As we saw in Table 2-1, shoppers in the convenience store channel exhibit strong variation in frequency, best customers shopping several times per week, lower value customers shopping intermittently.

Let's look at Report 2-3. In this example drawn from a specialty retailer, we are looking at three customer segments ranked by spending; the bottom 30% of customers, the top 10% of customers, and the top 1% of customers. We can see that there is a difference in the average selling price per item, ranging from nearly $4.50 to slightly over $6.00, an increase of 38% from the bottom 30% of customers to the top 1%.

Report 2-3

Specialty Retailers			
Customers Ranked by Spending	Bottom 30% of Customers	Top 10% of Customers	Top 1% of Customers
Average Selling Price per Item	$4.48	$6.14	$6.17
# of Items per Visit	1.74	6.4	7.8
Visits per Year	4.2	21	35.5
Annualized Sales per Customer	$32.76	$825.30	$1,708.62

When viewing the average quantity of items purchased in a shopping trip we begin to see stronger differences in shopping behavior appear. The lowest spending customers purchase less than two items per visit; the top customers purchase almost eight items each trip. Now though, let's look at shopping frequency. We see that the top group of customers shop approximately three times per month (35.5 times per year); the lower spending segment of customers is shopping only 0.35 times per month (4.2 visits per year).

Carrying our calculations further, we see that the annualized value of the best customer segment is over 52 times greater than the least valuable customers. This is one of the reasons why retailers must look beyond gross averages; without exception, every retail channel we have studied exhibits large differences in the value of the retailer's customers.

In the two following reports we can see customer shopping data from additional channels; fast food operators and book stores. Each of these retail sectors also exhibit strong differences in customer value.

In fast food establishments we see similar trends; the highest spending customers shopping on a much more frequent basis and having a higher average spend per visit than the lower spending segments. In this example, the highest spending customers are visiting over 88 times per year compared to less than two trips per year amongst the bottom 10% of customers. The highest value fast food customers are generating nearly 100 times the sales of the lowest spending customers.

Fast Food Operators

Decile	Average Spend Per Year	Avg. # Transactions Per Year	Avg. Spend Per Transaction
10	$523.11	88.8	$5.89
9	$260.58	46.3	$5.63
8	$178.24	32.8	$5.43
7	$128.23	24.5	$5.23
6	$92.09	18	$5.12
5	$65.06	13.1	$4.97
4	$43.99	9	$4.89
3	$27.48	5.9	$4.66
2	$14.79	3.3	$4.48
1	$5.32	1.6	$3.33

* Data provided by Visible Results (www.visibleresults.com)

Bookstores

Decile	Average Spend Per Year	Avg. # Transactions Per Year	Avg. Spend Per Transaction
10	$1,126.08	17.5	$64.35
9	$550.28	11	$50.03
8	$384.98	8.3	$46.38
7	$281.15	6.5	$43.25
6	$214.76	5.2	$41.30
5	$163.36	4.1	$39.84
4	$119.53	3.2	$37.35
3	$82.75	2.5	$33.10
2	$52.38	1.8	$29.10
1	$27.77	1.4	$19.84

* Data provided by Visible Results (www.visibleresults.com)

Bookstore customers exhibit great variation in their shopping behavior as well. We see the same trends in this channel as others; greater frequency and larger transaction sizes as we move up the customer segments.

Some readers may be tempted to explain away the differences in these examples by assuming that the highest spending customers are identifying themselves every time they shop and the lowest spending customers are only identifying themselves occasionally while actually shopping more often, thus leading to these discrepancies in spending. This argument rapidly loses strength in retail companies that accurately identify upwards of 85% or 90% of their total purchases to individual customers. There is indeed great variation in customer value.

Customer Profitability

While much has been accomplished using customer value derived from purchasing and frequency, leading companies desired an even more in-depth view; moving from viewing customer purchasing to customer profitability.

In many retail channels, the practice of high-low marketing is well ingrained. By this, I mean that a retailer will place a regular price on products but then periodically place specified products on sale at a lower deal price for a limited period of time. Supermarket flyers are a prime example of this type of marketing, as are department store sales, chain drug store flyers, and so on. This type of marketing results in the retailer incurring a markdown expense representing the cost of their price reductions; this is typically a major expense item for retailers, but one that many do not track and measure accurately. And it is this area that provides fertile breeding grounds for vast differences in consumer shopping behavior.

At this stage, most mass retailers do not have accurate item level cost information that can be easily attributed to a transaction log, thus allowing a true measure of customer profitability. This is an especially daunting challenge in the supermarket channel, where perishable foods sold by random weight (meats, produce, etc.) combine with product shrink (foods that spoil and have to be thrown out) to make it very difficult to derive a true product cost on many items that are sold.

Drawing information from Report 2-2, which presented the differences in customer shopping behavior found in a supermarket company, we will insert an additional two columns to create Report 2-6; the first reporting the specific markdown (or discount) dollars each decile of customers received, and the second reporting the percentage of the retailer's total markdown expense realized by each customer grouping. As we can see, the top 10% of customers (ranked by spending) generated nearly 60% of sales yet received only 48% of the total markdown expenditure. Contrast that finding with the customers of the third decile who provided 0.8% of total sales yet received 1.4% of the retailer's total markdown expenditure. These are actual numbers drawn from a retailer's database and provide a real world example of the discontinuity between customer value and marketing expenditures.

Report 2-6

Decile Report With Corresponding Markdown Expense

Decile	# of Customers	Decile Spending	% of Total	Decile Markdown $	% of Total Markdown
10	2,671	$10,161,647.00	59.4%	$813,439.00	48.2%
9	2,671	$3,113,702.00	18.2%	$326,487.00	19.3%
8	2,671	$1,564,890.00	9.1%	$188,791.00	11.2%
7	2,671	$891,308.00	5.2%	$116,982.00	6.9%
6	2,671	$544,806.00	3.4%	$107,742.00	6.4%
5	2,671	$345,851.00	2.0%	$52,698.00	3.1%
4	2,671	$218,307.00	1.3%	$35,685.00	2.1%
3	2,671	$132,857.00	0.8%	$23,580.00	1.4%
2	2,671	$73,003.00	0.4%	$15,051.00	0.9%
1	2,671	$27,984.00	0.2%	$7,984.00	0.5%
Total	**26,710**	**$17,074,355.00**	**100.00%**	**$1,688,439.00**	**100%**

There is an additional way to express the data to better show the disparity between customer spending and the discounts received. In Report 2-7 we are showing the markdown received by each decile as a percentage of the customers' total spending. For example, we can see that for the top decile of customers, markdown equates to 8% of total purchasing; for the bottom decile it equates to over 28% of the total, a vast difference. Use of this metric becomes important later in that this ratio becomes indicative of shopping motivation; is the customer deal-driven or relationship-driven?

Report 2-7

Markdown Relative to Customer Spending

Decile	Decile Spending	% of Total	Decile Markdown $	Markdown as % of Spending
10	$10,161,647.00	59.4%	$813,439.00	8.0%
9	$3,113,702.00	18.2%	$326,487.00	10.5%
8	$1,564,890.00	9.1%	$188,791.00	12.1%
7	$891,308.00	5.2%	$116,982.00	13.1%
6	$544,806.00	3.4%	$77,408.00	14.2%
5	$345,851.00	2.0%	$52,698.00	15.2%
4	$218,307.00	1.3%	$35,685.00	16.3%
3	$132,857.00	0.8%	$23,580.00	17.7%
2	$73,003.00	0.4%	$15,051.00	20.6%
1	$27,984.00	0.2%	$7,984.00	28.5%
Total	**$17,074,355.00**	**100%**	**$1,688,439.00**	**9.9%**

We can graphically express this misalignment between a retailer's customer base and the company's marketing expenditures. In the following illustration, the pyramid on the left represents a retailer's customer base. The top of the pyramid represents a company's best customers, those providing a large share of the annual turnover. The bottom portion of the pyramid represents those customers who account for a very small portion of the retailer's sales over time.

The pyramid on the right represents the sum value of a company's marketing expenditures, including mass media and promotions. Often a retail company's price reduction expense is a significant part of the company's total marketing expenditures. We see that in traditional retail economics, the retailer's most valuable customers receive a disproportionately small share of a retailer's marketing funds, the least valuable customers receiving an outsized share.

Traditional Retail Marketing Economics

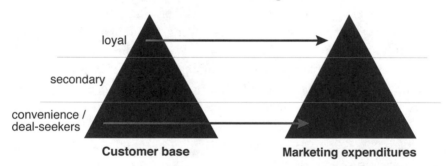

loyal

secondary

convenience /
deal-seekers

Customer base   **Marketing expenditures**

We can further our understanding of customer value by distilling the information shown in Report 2-7 and appending another two columns to create Report 2-8. Before proceeding, the retailer must understand how they report sales in their financial reporting. For decades, the common practice has been to report sales net of markdown expenditure. In a very real sense, this practice has set the stage for many retailers to not truly understand their total marketing expenditures; by not tracking their price reduction expense on their profit and loss statements, companies were oblivious to a very substantial cost figure. Retailers that are able to track their total markdown expense through their POS systems now have a choice; they can continue to report net sales on their management reporting (thus ignoring their markdown expense), or they can report their true (gross) sales and treat their price reduction number as the marketing expense that it really is. Either way, the retailer with the necessary information can compute customer profit margins and begin to understand customer profitability.

Report 2-8

		Projected Customer Profitability				
Decile	# of Customers	Decile Spending	Decile Markdown $	Markdown as % of Spending	Company GPM %	Margin Net of Markdown Expense
10	2,671	$10,161,647.00	$813,439.00	8.0%	38%	30.0%
9	2,671	$3,113,702.00	$326,487.00	10.5%	38%	27.5%
8	2,671	$1,564,890.00	$188,791.00	12.1%	38%	25.9%
7	2,671	$891,308.00	$116,982.00	13.1%	38%	24.9%
6	2,671	$544,806.00	$107,742.00	19.8%	38%	18.2%
5	2,671	$345,851.00	$52,698.00	15.2%	38%	22.8%
4	2,671	$218,307.00	$35,685.00	16.3%	38%	21.7%
3	2,671	$132,857.00	$23,580.00	17.7%	38%	20.3%
2	2,671	$73,003.00	$15,051.00	20.6%	38%	17.4%
1	2,671	$27,984.00	$7,984.00	28.5%	38%	9.5%
Total	26,710	$17,074,355.00	$1,688,439.00	9.9%	38%	28.1%

In this report we are using an assumed company gross margin of 38%. For companies not able to measure true customer profitability based upon item purchases we can apply an assumed gross, using the company's overall gross profit margin prior to markdown expense. With the proper data, we could report the actual gross margin realized from each decile of customers prior to markdown. For purposes of our illustration either method is acceptable for bringing to light the vast differences in customer value.

What this report tells us is that the top 10% of customers are generating an estimated 30% gross profit margin, net of markdown expenditures, while the bottom 10% of customers are generating less than 10% margin net of markdown. Assuming this company's cost of operations is 25%, a substantial part of his customer base is generating a margin less than needed to cover the cost of providing service to them.

Yield Management

In another sense, this retailer's most valuable customers are generating enough profit to cover the retailer's fixed overhead, the lower value customers providing incremental profit from which only the incremental added costs of servicing them would need to be subtracted. This view is akin to the airline companies' practice of yield management; full price business travelers bearing the costs of the flight and the remaining seats sold at discounted prices to recreational travelers so as to fill the plane and generate incremental revenue.

Yield management is predicated on a simple principle: once fixed costs are covered, any additional revenue need only exceed the added incremental costs of servicing the incremental business to add to profitability.

But yield management as practiced by airline companies also warns of potential dangers for the retail world. The practice of yield management grew from a historical view of airline travel; the airlines saw that a majority of travelers were business people and the airlines additionally saw that some portion of seats on many flights went empty. The airline companies then reasoned that by offering deeply discounted fares on some seats, they might be able to persuade recreational travelers to fly, thus filling the previously empty seats and generating more revenue per flight.

Implicit in this rationale was the assumption that customer behavior would not change, that the business travelers were hostage to their schedules and would continue to pay full regular fare.[1] As the airline companies have discovered, this was a dangerous assumption to rely upon as more and more business travelers are no longer tolerating exorbitant prices and are changing their schedules to take advantage of the discounted fares or avoiding air travel altogether and making use of videoconferencing.

Customers are human beings that learn behaviors. Companies practicing yield management, like the airlines, teach consumers to pursue low prices. Such companies set in motion a cycle through which their revenue per customer begins to decline as more and more customers search out lower and lower fares. The department store channel provides a good example of this in practice; consumers now wait until the department stores offer massive markdowns before making their holiday purchases. The department store companies are caught in a cycle of having to bear more and more markdown cost to generate comparable same store sales volumes year to year.

We can transfer this yield management concept to the retail world. It is common practice for supermarket retailers to put "loss leaders" on the front page of their flyers, products sold at a pure loss in hopes of luring customers to the store. Time and again in studying customer data generated within traditional supermarket environments, we have found some segment of consumers who simply purchase the loss leaders and proceed out the door, leaving the store with an outright loss on the transaction.

Now, every retail store must pay utilities, meet payroll, and afford other business expenses. Where do such monies come from if some customers are generating a financial loss for the store? The profits to pay expenses are being derived from the regular loyal patrons (analogous to the airline business travelers)—who are also subsidizing the "cherry-pickers", those consumers only purchasing deal-priced merchandise (those travelers lured by discounted fares). In effect, supermarket companies have been unconsciously practicing yield management. It is only with the view made possible by customer information that the companies could see actual customer behavior. A similar environment exists in other sectors, such as department stores, discount stores, chain drug stores, etc.; any retail company going to market with a high-low pricing philosophy.

This type of analysis begins bringing to light the importance of a relatively small number of highly profitable customers, those customer households that have an enormous impact on the profitability of a company. Many retailers working with customer data routinely refer to the top 30% of customers (when ranked by spending) as their best customers and focus their efforts on these people. While this is important, the true power resides in a small group of customers within the top 30%. Additionally, as some retailers have been aware of for some time, retailers going to market with a high-low pricing philosophy can have within their ranks high spending, but low profit, customers; the deal seekers, who, though they are spending a high number of dollars, purchase most everything on sale. This is why actual customer profitability has become so sought after.

While even this analysis is relatively advanced for practitioners of customer intelligence, the bar is being raised yet again. A small handful of retail companies have put systems and processes into place so that they are now able to measure actual customer profitability, built from item level purchases up to the customer's total spending and gross profit. This area has become the Holy Grail for retailers working with retail customer data. And for good reason: actual customer profitability removes the last vestiges of fogginess from the view of a retail business. Management now has a complete understanding of not only which categories and products account for their profits, but a knowledge of which customers generate those product purchases.

The Wisdom of Time

But even viewing actual customer profitability does not provide the complete story. To retailers operating in the world of customer intelligence, time is as important a factor in determining customer value as spending, frequency, and profit margin.

We live in a very fast-paced world by historical standards. Increasingly, people have shown a proclivity for more immediate gratification, shunning delayed rewards. Such pressures have created a substantial alteration in the time perspectives management must deal with, both in terms of marketing to consumers as well as internal management goals and objectives.

Management has more and more been forced into making decisions to bolster short term results, sometimes at the expense of long term benefit. One cannot overly fault such management decisions; indeed, meeting or exceeding quarterly projections has become the expected behavior given the reward structure of Wall Street and financial institutions. This is not far different than retailers driving advertised specials to even lower price points so as to generate sales, the profitability of those sales open to question.

To fully appreciate the perspective of time relative to customer value we must look far beyond a single transaction, and even beyond the sum of a customer's transactions over a quarter, or even a year.

As mentioned earlier, Green Hills is a large independent supermarket. Green Hills began collecting detailed customer information at the launch of their loyalty platform in early 1993 and has been adding to it ever since. Green Hills is unique in that it has more than a decade's worth of customer level shopping data in its database, thus allowing the measurement of customer behavior over years. The store is an exception in this regard, as most retail companies of any size that capture detailed customer information tend to maintain only one to two years of data prior to archiving, thus limiting the view of customer behavior over time to these companies.

So what do we learn by exploring the shopping behavior of Green Hills' customers over a long period? We will use a five year period of time, from January 1, 1997 through December 31, 2001, drawn from a study Green Hills did of long term customer behavior. During that five year period, Green Hills had 28,748 unique customer households shopping. The study focused on the top 10% of households ranked by spending, or 2,875 customer households, during the study period.

Lisa Piron, Director of Information Systems for Green Hills, and responsible for the analysis, found that of those 2,875 households, 95% of them (2,736) shopped each year during the five year period; these customers shopped, on average, between 1.5 and 4.3 times per week during the five years. Further, this small handful of customers generated 64% of total identified sales for the entire five year period (Green Hills identifies 90% of total sales through its loyalty platform). Individual customer spending for the five years ranged from $7,000 to over $85,000 during the study period.

Piron drilled down even further to focus on the top 1% of customer households, again ranked by spending, during the five year period. These 270 customer households generated over 21% of total identified sales during the five years.

Brian Woolf, in his work in supermarket retailing, has identified the great amount of fluctuation that occurs amongst higher spending customers when viewed quarter to quarter. He has found that a significant number of customers who are ranked as best customers in one period decline in spending to a lower level during the following period; others rising to take their place. [2]

The work done at Green Hills carries this discovery further. By looking at customer behavior over much longer periods of time, we have found that a relatively small number of customers provide very substantial portions of the total sales over time. But what is surprising is that some of these very valuable customers do not necessarily show up when doing more traditional best customer types of analysis, such as looking at the top 10-20% of customers during a given quarter. These long term, highly valuable patrons are many times hidden just beneath the surface, oftentimes not recognized by best customer programs focused on short time periods.

Traditional "Best Customer" discovery
Short time periods (e.g. Quarter) high spending

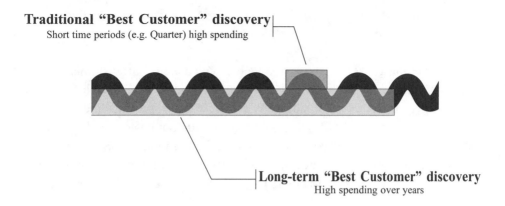

Long-term "Best Customer" discovery
High spending over years

For a better understanding of this concept, imagine a retailer's customer base being akin to the water in a lake. The fluctuation in customer spending over time can be represented by waves rolling over the surface. Traditional best customer segmentations typically look at customer spending behavior over relatively short periods of time (months, quarters, even a year); this period of time likened to the crest of the wave, that portion of the wave above the average water level. Long term best customers many times occupy the space just beneath the wave crest; sometimes they get caught up in the crest and are recognized as best customers, but many times they are residing just beneath the surface, always present but sometimes not recognized due the cresting behavior of other customers over short periods.

This is an important discovery in customer value and shopping behavior over time. This finding opens yet another dimension in retail battles and only companies amassing detailed customer data over time can enter the fray. The knowledge that some customers in retail generate thousands of times more in sales and profits over their consumer lifetime than other consumers stands in stark contrast to the usual short term perspective held by many firms. It will be interesting to see how public retail companies reconcile their quarter-to-quarter financial perspective with the need to recognize and market to consumer behavior when measured in years.

The concept of taking a long-term perspective when measuring customer value speaks to another concept: customer lifetime value. In researching the concept and calculation of customer lifetime value, one finds quite a number of differing theories and measures. Many times loyalty practitioners calculate customer lifetime value based upon spending and customer retention measures; if accurate gross profit margin information is available, this can be factored in as well.

To illustrate the power of time, one retailer calculated that customers in the company's highest spending customer segment had a lifetime value of over $17,000 per customer. The company's lowest spending customer segment produced a lifetime value of only slightly over $300 per customer. If you were this retailer, where would you invest your marketing monies? Such measures strongly suggest the importance of retaining the most valuable customers over time, as well as attempting to create more such customers within a company's customer base.

What has been lacking in this measure is a way to relate it back to existing measures of retail financial performance. While it makes logical sense that by improving customer retention or customer spending, and thereby increasing the lifetime value of a certain portion of a retailer's customer base, it is difficult to relate this back to the financial statements each period. In a stable environment in which all mitigating factors are removed from the equation, it would be much easier to equate improvements in customer lifetime value to actual financial performance. Unfortunately, the real world does not allow us to control many of the other factors which can impact on sales and profitability; the world of retail is far too dynamic, both in terms of consumer behavior and relative to competitive activities.

For retail companies building their customer data repositories over years of time, it is far more practical to measure the behavior of the different segments of customers as they gradually emerge. Loyalty can be defined in terms of spending and shopping behavior over time. It follows, then, as Green Hills found in its analysis, that loyal customers can be defined as those that are higher spending when viewed over relatively short periods of time, or customers at a somewhat lower spending level but consistent in their shopping over long periods of time. This lengthening of time when valuing customers provides a new competitive arena, retail companies able to discover and working to retain customers over years and decades of time.

Differentiation

So now that we have an understanding of the vast differences in customer shopping behavior, and the resulting differences in customer economic value, where do we go next?

Customer intelligent retail companies have pulled this understanding of variations in customer value into all parts of their organization, using it to align decision making with those customers offering the highest (or highest potential) value to the company. By aligning merchandising and operations with preferences exhibited by the higher value customer segments, retail companies can begin the process of improving retention of these worthy customers over time, realize even more purchasing from them, and begin to attract other, similar, high value customers. As this occurs, substantial increases in sales and profitability soon follow. This is the essence of a customer intelligent business strategy.

Once retail companies understand this difference in value amongst their customer base, it is difficult to turn back. Retailers understand and accept that many times the different products and services they sell all generate varying amounts of profitability, but this does not mean that retailers do not actively try and work their product mix to improve their yield or profitability. The same analogy can be applied to customers; retailers can significantly improve their yield by differentiating between customers and improve the company's profitability.

While this and many other arguments promoting the practice of differentiation between customers to improve financial results are logical in a financial sense, there is perhaps another, more visceral reason that retail companies should consider pursuing this direction.

Many retailers, including some of the largest, consider themselves "agents" for their customers; operating with the philosophy that customers are entrusting the company with their monies and that their job, as the retailer, is to supply the best value possible to their customers. [3] Now put this agentry philosophy in terms of the preceding discussion of customer profitability; should a retailer acting as agent for his customers allow some portion of those loyal customers' spending to go towards subsidizing the "deal-only" customers? As a life-long retail merchant, I believe that my best customers, those who have shopped with me for years, should receive the best value, not the cherry-pickers who come once for a sale product and are never seen again.

Some consumer advocates say that it is discriminatory for supermarkets to link their lowest prices to the company's loyalty card, feeling it pressures consumers to forfeit their privacy (by having to sign up for the program) so as to receive the deals. But is it fair that a store's regular patrons are, in effect, paying extra to finance the customer who goes store to store purchasing the loss leaders?

This is an important point in the ongoing debate over loyalty programs. Outside observers question the value of price-based loyalty programs (as are common in the supermarket channel) when comparing prices with mass merchants selling the same products without a card program. These critics miss the fundamental point of loyalty programs: correctly done, retail loyalty programs provide a way for a company to shift their values and rewards from immediate gratification (transaction-based discounts) to long term rewards based upon the customer's shopping over time.

I will be the first to state that retailers instituting some type of customer information gathering platform, but then do nothing to reward or recognize their regular patrons, should terminate their efforts; the retailer is offering no advantage to consumers for joining and using their frequent shopper cards. Retailers guilty of this practice are requiring more from the consumer without providing any benefit in return, further penalizing those customers not joining.

Customer intelligent retailers now have a way to direct their values and financial rewards to those customers regularly shopping with the company, rather than providing heavily discounted prices to anyone walking in the door. Leading practitioners of customer intelligent retailing work to create a true win-win relationship with their regular customers, providing their valuable patrons with improved benefits over time.

Manufacturers Gathering Data

Beyond this, what other reasons exist for retail companies to begin collecting, understanding, and using customer data? There is an additional movement in the retail industry that should be addressed here: the fact that more and more manufacturers, suppliers to the retail industry, are aggressively increasing their efforts at developing consumer level data.

Procter & Gamble executed an online marketing campaign to promote its Tide Kick stain pre-treating product, offering free samples to households that supplied their contact information. The program generated over three million requests for a free sample from U.S. consumers, giving Procter & Gamble over three million customer names and addresses (and e-mails!) to add to their already massive consumer database. [4]

Dole recently announced the launch of a consumer rewards program, DOLE myGREEN$. Inside specially marked bags of Dole salad mix the consumer will find coupon booklets with a unique code for $10 in shopping credit at different online retailers. To redeem, consumers must register on the Dole website and enter the code; Dole gets customer names and contact data. [5]

Kraft has one of, if not the largest, consumer databases in the world, actively seeking consumer level contact information through a variety of channels from sweepstakes to call centers.

Such customer data gathering schemes exist far beyond the food and consumer packaged goods industries. Warranty registrations for electronics or appliances provide consumer contact data to the manufacturer. Across a great number of channels, activities such as mail-in rebates, product registrations, sweepstakes, and other vehicles, all provide for ways of gathering end-customer contact information for the manufacturers of the goods.

While it is impractical to sell many consumer packaged goods products or other merchandise directly to the consumer, this does not preclude the manufacturer from attempting to usurp the retailer's traditional role; that of having the relationship with the end customer. Manufacturers time and again are pursuing consumer level data so as to learn more of customers' shopping behavior, but to also begin fostering a relationship directly with the consumer.

Retailers must remember that, while manufacturers are a key component of the industry supply chain, at the end of the day the agenda of the manufacturer is quite different from that of the retailer. The manufacturer is concerned only with the goal of having consumers purchase their branded goods; it does not matter at which store the consumer does the purchasing. Conversely, many times the retailer is not overly concerned with which specific product or brand a consumer buys, as long as it is at their store and not a competitor's.

I shall never forget a meeting I had some time ago with several brand managers for one of the largest consumer packaged goods companies relative to customer data in retail. After I had delivered a presentation on the types of information leading retailers were capturing, how the data was being structured, and how it was being used, the brand managers were aghast. There was great fear that as retailers truly began to understand which products their most valuable customers were purchasing, and how shopping behavior could be altered through changing the reward structure, that the consumer packaged goods companies would be in much weaker negotiating positions with the larger retailers. These brand managers understood that information is power; he that controls (and uses) the information (customer data) is in the strongest position.

A similar view is put forth in a report issued by Cap Gemini Ernst & Young. The report, "State of the Art in Food: The Changing Face of the Food Industry", suggests that leading manufacturers are aware of the need to create strong brands and relationships with consumers. As such, some manufacturers are seeking to market directly to consumers, bypassing retailers. A majority of manufacturers surveyed report they fear the consequences of the retail channel gaining strength. [6]

The Power of Personalization

Yet another reason building the case for retailers to capture, understand, and use customer data in how they go to market is drawn from looking at other businesses consumers do business with. Technology is increasingly leading to a world in which consumers are expecting to have their preferences known by companies they do business with. Hertz maintains detailed records of customer preferences for its Hertz #1 Club Gold members; the customer only has to request a reservation by phone or via the company's website, and all details such as car preference, smoking or non-smoking vehicle, and so on are already noted. Hotels are also building such records. I have only to call the Ritz Carlton Hotel in Chicago and identify myself by name, the reservations person immediately seeing my room preferences, including room size, floor, and other amenities in their database.

Personalization in consumer business transactions is rapidly becoming the order of the day enabled by the internet. Lands' End offers custom made pants through its web site, allowing customers to choose fabrics, styles and colors. The company states that 40% of jean and chino sales are custom orders. Nike enables customers to customize sneakers through its website; 20% of web sales are customized products. Procter & Gamble, through its Reflect.com internet company, provides cosmetics customized to the individual based upon the customer answering questions about skin type and other factors. Procter & Gamble states that 75% to 80% of sales through Reflect.com are customized. [7]

These trends in consumer products perhaps owe their beginnings to Dell Computer, the king of made-to-order personal computers. Dell's success has led Apple Computer, Gateway, Hewlett-Packard, and IBM to offer customized personal computers online. Even the car business is moving in this direction. Ford related websites letting consumers choose the color and other features of a car, the data then forwarded on to a local dealer to locate or order the car for the customer. [8]

Consumers will expect no less in a retail setting, anticipating that the department store will know which clothing lines they are interested in purchasing and even the sizes required. Prada is working to create the retail store of the future in its New York city flagship store. Using radio frequency tags, associates are able to access store inventory through a handheld unit. Customers are able to receive cards that detail past purchases and contain notes store associates have made about their purchases. Customers can also begin building a "virtual closet" and store information about purchases in an internet-based account. [9]

While we will address successful practices more specifically and provide examples of customer intelligence strategy at work further on in the book, there are two additional topics which must be addressed prior to proceeding. The issues of differentiation amongst customers and the confidentiality of consumer data are critical to any customer intelligent retail company.

Retailing has traditionally been a very egalitarian environment with regard to the service and product pricing extended to customers. Who has not heard over and over that in retailing "the customer is always right" or "treat every customer as you would want to be treated"? Companies of any size realize that they must provide strong customer service to any customer in order to avoid offending someone, thereby generating poor word of mouth publicity. But one must wonder if retailing would have evolved so had early mass retailers known the economic value of their various customers.

Perhaps by studying other businesses that provide goods or services direct to consumers we can add to our understanding of the philosophical debate in retail relative to differentiating between customers. Anyone who has flown on a commercial airline within the past decade has most likely experienced a form of customer differentiation in practice. One of the benefits provided flyers who achieve a specified number of miles with an airline is that of early boarding of the aircraft, a provided privilege intended to allow the frequent traveler to find room for their carry on bags.

Who has not spent time waiting in line at a popular restaurant, only to see someone enter, proceed to the host or hostess, and receive their table seating on a moment's notice? More times than not, this is best customer marketing at work, albeit on a more informal basis; well run restaurants are very aware of their frequent patrons and make certain that they are well provided for.

Frequent travelers have come to expect, indeed have been taught, to expect special treatment, be it special check-in lines at the airport, hotel room upgrades, or Hertz's practice of having their valued customer's rental car waiting with the heater running during winter or the air conditioning in warmer climates. Consumers are not automatons, adhering to regular behaviors in their shopping patterns regardless of the service experience they receive. More and more people are expecting, if not demanding, recognition and special attention at businesses they frequent.

Consumers today are much more comfortable with the concept of differentiation than they were perhaps a decade ago. The recognition of regular customers has become much more commonplace—be it when flying, staying in a hotel, renting a car, or buying groceries. Many times consumers not only accept the notion of differentiation, but the more astute customers are now expecting a company to know that they are a good customer and treat them accordingly.

Almost all retailers who begin to understand the differences in valuation amongst their customers soon grapple with the philosophical debate of whether or not, and if so, how much, to differentiate between their individual customers. There is no right or wrong answer; the correct solution is one fitting to the particular retailer, a solution that fits with their company culture, one that management and staff are comfortable executing on the sales floor. Time and again I have seen management intellectually understand the need for customer differentiation when in their offices, yet become tongue-tied when confronted by a customer on the sales floor who questions why they have not received some best customer perquisite.

The practice of such differentiation is not so much meant to financially penalize lower spending customers as it is to recognize and reward those shopping on a regular basis with the retailer and providing the majority of the company's income. Perhaps rather than continue presenting the concept of differentiation as a good customer / bad customer debate, retail executives can begin to reframe the discussion, approaching differentiation as supporting a more customer specific marketing approach. Technology is readily making practical the extension of various offers to individual customers; the mix of offers and information tailored to the customer's preferences as gleaned from historical purchasing activity or timing of certain purchases. Posed this way, differentiation should be an acceptable practice to most anyone, as most consumers will gain through receiving offers of value directed to them individually.

In some cases, having consumer data provides additional safety margins. There have been a number of cases in food retailing where companies have searched their transaction databases to identify customers who purchased some product that has been recalled, or possibly tainted. This practice is not far different from automobile manufacturers contacting consumers who they know own a certain vehicle to inform them of possible safety hazards or recalls. Think of the toy retailer able to identify purchasers of a certain baby toy being recalled for safety reasons.

Confidentiality

As the practice of collecting customer data grows and expands throughout retailing, periodic concerns over the confidentiality of such data have washed through the media.

The supermarket industry in particular has an exemplary record of protecting the confidentiality of their customers' data. I am not aware of even one case of a supermarket retailer in the U.S. selling, trading, or in any way making available customer contact information to any manufacturer, advertising firm, direct marketing agency, or anyone outside of the retailer's company. Contrast this, though, with the behavior of other types of business having far more confidential, and potentially threatening, customer information. Banks and credit card companies have sold consumer data for years to various marketing and rating agencies. Direct mail publications and magazine companies have sold customer contact lists whenever and wherever possible. And, the height of hypocrisy, a number of different states continued to sell driver license data to outside organizations until recently.

At a more philosophical level, what is transpiring is a value exchange between the retailer and the consumer. The retailer is offering the consumer some value (which can take many forms as we shall see) in exchange for the consumer identifying themselves each time they shop, thus providing detailed shopping data.

This type of value exchange, information for some type of value, goes on constantly. Any time a person applies for life insurance they must provide intimate details of their lives and financial state. Whenever someone applies for automobile insurance, a background check is done to check for driving records, previous accidents, speeding tickets and such. And whenever someone applies for a credit card or bank loan, they must open up their entire financial history to a stranger. But people are willing to do this, indeed usually do not even think twice about doing this, because they need the service or product in return.

Consumers have regularly engaged in a value exchange, trading their privacy or information for some type of value. Consumers don't think twice about making a telephone call, yet a record is maintained of all calls made. Personal checks, credit cards, and debit cards all provide a value and convenience to the consumer; yet, all provide for a loss of anonymity.

To be successful, retailers must never lose sight of the trust and relationship they have with their customers. Detailed shopping information must be treated with the highest level of concern for the privacy of our customers.

CLOSING THE LOOP

During a conversation one day with an industry executive, I was asked why more retail companies were not making use of the data gathered through their frequent shopper programs. While there exist numerous challenges related to the gathering, understanding, and use of customer data in a retail setting, the largest obstacle lies in how customer data is structured and organized.

Senior executives rely upon financial reporting for gauging the health of their companies. Profit and loss statements and balance sheets list tangible assets; sales are stated based upon the exact movement of hard products at specified prices. Inventories reflect the value of (amongst other things) the products sitting on the shelf or in the back room awaiting sale. The value of a certain product is the cost of what it was purchased for; specific, unambiguous black and white data.

Customer reporting, on the other hand, is often viewed by management as the antithesis of financial reporting. Customer-based data is seen as interesting, possibly of use in the marketing department or in the real estate department to assist in site selection, but that's about it. Customer data is nebulous, not hard and defined as product-based data is. Yes, executives may say, I understand that the top 30% of my customers generate 75% of my sales, but how is that going to help me hit my sales budget for next period or my bottom line?

Customer Tier Management...

"Ahhh, Hawkins-san, you are describing moving from relative measures to absolute measures!" With that comment, John Okazaki, former President of The Continuity Company of Japan, neatly summarized the distinction between viewing customer data as appropriate for marketing initiatives and the use of customer data as a hard-edged business metric. Management and financial reporting must be comprised of absolute numbers, not percentage-based relative measures that ebb and flow.

Imagine joining an airline frequent flyer program and being told that to qualify for the Gold tier you must be in the top 10% of flying customers that month. That's fine, but what does that mean in specific terms of the number of miles you must fly? The top 10% mileage threshold may be one number one month and another number the next month because it is a relative measure; the specific threshold number is dependent upon the relative performance of the other flyers. Far better for the airlines (as they do) to state that one must fly 50,000 miles each calendar year to qualify for Gold status.

To provide actionable information in the way they measure and manage their businesses, retailers have for years categorized their product or service offerings into departments or categories. They then periodically aggregate data back against these groupings to do financial reporting. Look at any retailer's profit and loss statement; inevitably it is broken down into product groupings that measure sales, margins, and applicable costs to create department or category level metrics. The retailer can now measure the different revenue and profit streams offered by the different product categories.

With customer tier management, we are working to create a reporting structure through which we can begin to track changes over time in the composition and behavior of a retailer's customer base; changes that have strong financial implications for profitability. This is done by using defined spending thresholds for specific time periods to segment customers. While the specific numbers used to create the different customer tiers will change by retail channel and monetary currency, the underlying concept remains the same: moving from relative, percentage-based measures to absolute measures of customer shopping behavior.

For our example we will use fictional data based upon a composite of retail stores, using four customer tiers predicated upon spending during a quarterly (13 week) financial period and a last segment for those sales unidentified to specific consumers:

Table 3-1

Tier 1: those customers spending over $1,000.00
Tier 2: those customers spending between $500.00 and $999.99
Tier 3: those customers spending between $250.00 and $499.99
Tier 4: those customers spending less than $249.99
Unidentified: those customers not identifying themselves during transaction
Spending thresholds based upon customer spend during a quarter (13 week period)

The spending thresholds used in this example are for purposes of illustration. The actual thresholds used by a retailer are dependent upon their customer shopping data; the segmentations must be meaningful for the retail channel and the individual retailer. For example, using a $1,000.00 spending threshold for a 13 week quarter may be appropriate for a supermarket retailer but would not be applicable to a bookstore as very few customers would likely spend that amount. Conversely, the $1,000 threshold for a Tier 1 customer would be inappropriate for a high end jeweler, having customers that spend many times that amount in one purchase.

Retailers moving in this direction should not be concerned with attempting to use channel-specific thresholds; the power of this type of segmenting lies in its use as an internal measurement, helping benchmark the retailer's own performance over time.

Using the segmentation criteria shown in Table 3-1 we can segment the customer data for the stated time period (13 weeks) and measure precisely the number of customer households which are in each segment and their related shopping behavior, as shown in Report 3-1.

Report 3-1

Sample Customer Tier Report

	Total	Tier 1	Tier 2	Tier 3	Tier 4	Unidentified
# of Customers	12,000	360	1,200	2,040	8,400	n/a
% of total identified	100%	3%	10%	17%	70%	n/a
Sales $	$3,000,000	$510,000	$960,000	$570,000	$720,000	$300,000
% of total	100%	17%	32%	19%	24%	10%
Avg. $ per Customer		$1,416.67	$800.00	$279.41	$85.71	n/a
Avg. # Visits		28.5	19.3	11.6	3.6	n/a
Avg. Transaction Size		$49.71	$41.45	$24.09	$23.81	?

Tier 1: those customers spending over $1,000.00
Tier 2: those customers spending between $500.00 and $999.99
Tier 3: those customers spending between $250.00 and $499.99
Tier 4: those customers spending less than $249.99
Unidentified: those customers not identifying themselves during transaction
Spending thresholds based upon customer spend during a quarter (13 week period)

By applying the spending criteria to the reporting period (13 week quarter), we can divide the 12,000 total customer households into their respective tiers. Once this is accomplished we can proceed to report other attributes of each tier, such as sales, and can further calculate additional measures such as the average spending per customer, shopping frequency, and average transaction size. These measures bring to light the substantial differences in value between customers.

We have seen a number of retailers organize customer segments based upon lifestyle groupings, or scoring customers based upon their purchasing activity in a store's various departments or categories. Such efforts are at heart marketing-based; the segmentations do not provide the tools needed by management to make use of customer information in a strategic fashion. Management the world over has sought to measure marketing programs and initiatives; with enough customer data, that day may be at hand.

The purpose of customer tier segmentations is to structure customer data so as to make it valuable as a business measure; while these segments may serve as a basis for marketing initiatives, they do not need to do so, as we will discuss in the following chapter. There must be made a clear distinction between customer tier segmentations for management reporting purposes and customer segmentations done for marketing purposes. Marketing segmentations are for playing the game; financial-based segmentations are for keeping score.

It is only with a customer tier structure, based purely upon customer spending in a specified time period, that we are able to truly measure the impact of marketing upon customer activity – which directly impacts upon company profitability. Experience has shown that management, once grasping the concept, understands the value in structuring data this way for use throughout the company. Additionally, retailers fully cognizant of this reporting method, and using it in a disciplined way in going to market, have superior financial results to those companies solely relying on marketing-based segmentation schemes.

With this style of reporting as a foundation, a retailer can now begin to understand customer profitability.

As was discussed earlier, relatively few retail companies worldwide have the capability to accurately measure true customer profitability built from item level purchases; this necessitates the retailer maintaining accurate cost and retail data for every item sold and appending it to every customer identified transaction, along with whatever discounts or markdown the customer received. A majority of retail establishments do, though, have the capability to track their price reduction, or markdown, expense. By being able to track their markdown expenditures retailers are able to begin computing implied customer profitability.

Appending markdown expense to the individual customer enables this valuable information to be integrated into reporting, providing a way to view the alignment between the revenue a customer segment is providing each period and the amount of marketing expenditures (in this case, markdown expense) each segment is receiving. As we see in Report 3-2, Tier 2 customers generated 32% of total sales during the reporting period and received 18% of markdown expense or discounts. It is in this way that retailers understanding and using this customer tier management reporting structure can make measurable decisions about how they direct, or re-direct, their marketing expenditures.

Sales are reported at the gross level, that is, sales prior to any price reductions or markdown. Applying the "gross" gross profit margin (again, the gross margin which would be reported were every product to be sold at full retail) to the gross sales, we can calculate the gross profit dollars for the customer tier. By subtracting the markdown expense from the gross profit dollars, we are able to express the gross profit margin net of markdown expense for each customer tier.

Viewing data such as the sample provided in Report 3-2 will inevitably lead executives to question how they can improve their business performance by increasing that portion of their sales derived from Tier 1 or Tier 2 customers, which offer superior profitability. In a sense, this is no different than executives examining their financial reports and discussing maximizing their yield through the increased selling of more profitable product lines.

This sample report is to provide the reader with the concept of including customer data into a company's financial reporting. Actual financial reporting would also include comparative results with the previous year or against budget; the same comparative measures would apply to customer data as well.

Report 3-2

Report Period: 02	Total	Tier 1 Customers	Tier 2 Customers	Tier 3 Customers	Tier 4 Customers	Unidentified Customers
ID Rates: % of Sales: 90% % of Transactions: 80%						
Households	**12,000**	**360**	**1,200**	**2,040**	**8,400**	**n/a**
% of Total	100%	3%	10%	17%	70%	n/a
# transactions	140,000	12,000	27,000	25,000	48,000	28,000
% of total transactions	100%	8.57%	19.29%	17.86%	34.29%	20.00%
visits per week		2.56	1.73	0.94	0.44	
Sales	**$3,000,000**	**$510,000**	**$960,000**	**$570,000**	**$720,000**	**$300,000**
% of Total	*100%*	*17%*	*32%*	*19%*	*24%*	*10%*
Gross Profit Margin $	*$1,050,000*	*$178,500*	*$336,000*	*$199,500*	*$252,000*	*$105,000*
GPM %	35%	35%	35%	35%	35%	35%
Markdown Expense	$250,000	$12,500	$45,000	$70,000	$122,500	0
% of Total Markdown	100%	5%	18%	28%	49%	0%
GPM% Net of Markdown	26.67%	33%	30%	23%	18%	35%
Expenses:						
Operating	*$320,000*	*$27,424*	*$61,728*	*$57,152*	*$109,728*	*$64,000*
Occupancy	*$180,000*	*$15,426*	*$34,722*	*$32,148*	*$61,722*	*$36,000*
Admin	*$90,000*	*$7,713*	*$17,361*	*$16,074*	*$30,861*	*$18,000*
Marketing	*$60,000*	*$5,142*	*$11,574*	*$10,716*	*$20,574*	*$12,000*
Net Profit $	$150,000	$110,295	$165,615	$13,410	-$93,385	-$25,000
Net Profit %	**5%**	**21.63%**	**17.25%**	**2.35%**	**-12.97%**	**-8.33%**

N.B.: Notice the much higher gross profit margin realized by the unidentified customer tier. This example assumes the retailer is using a price-based loyalty platform in which all reduced prices require the retailer's loyalty card; thus, customers not using a card (unidentified) pay regular price. However, this does not mean that we wish to increase sales to the unidentified customers!

N.B.: In the above report, expenses have been prorated to each customer tier based upon the number of transactions reported. For example, Unidentified Customers accounted for 20% of total transactions; therefore 20% of the total operating expense is allocated to this Tier. This is for illustration purposes only; each retail company will have their own way of representing this type of information.

The variation in gross profit margin net of markdown expense shown in this example is not atypical of retail companies using a high-low pricing philosophy that we have studied. As was discussed earlier, such pricing methods create great variation in customer value, there being a wide range in the gross margin of products or services sold. For example, in the supermarket sector, using this method we regularly see a variation between 10% and 15% in the margin offered by Tier 1 customers and those in Tier 4. This margin spread is driven by differences in purchasing mix and the disproportionate amounts of the retailer's markdown expense going to the respective customer tiers. As we see in Report 3-2, Tier 1 customers are much higher spending; they are using the retailer as their primary store within the channel, purchasing many products at full retail price. Tier 4 customers are shopping the retailer out of convenience, or, as evidenced by the high amount of markdown accrued the customers in Tier 4, many of them shopping only for deal merchandise.

To more clearly demonstrate the significant differences in profitability generated by the customer tiers, it is possible to allocate some portion of expenses back to the customer tier, as shown in the sample statement. For this example we are allocating expenses to each customer tier based upon the number and percentage of total transactions each tier generates. Because we do not know the number of customers in the unidentified tier, we cannot base the allocation on numbers of customer households. Allocating costs based upon sales also has limitations in that much of the company's overhead (fixed cost structure) must be incurred regardless of the purchase amount of any given transaction. Some retail companies may wish to prorate costs based upon the number of items purchased. What is important is the concept of integrating customer metrics into a company's financial reporting system.

This exercise provides a new perspective on retail operations and marketing methods. This level of information again highlights the profound variances in customer value found in the typical retail store and again clearly demonstrates the fact that a retailer's higher spending (higher value) customers subsidize the lower spending customers (convenience customers or deal seekers). Many retail executives, when first seeing such information drawn from their own companies, experience an epiphany; the light finally dawning as to the reasons for capturing and using customer information.

Typically, we suggest aligning customer reporting with a company's financial reporting, thus making the eventual integration of the two somewhat easier. Incorporating customer-based metrics into a retailer's financial reporting also stresses the value of these metrics to others in the organization. Top management will now be viewing on a regular basis how well the company is doing in terms of retaining customers, and will begin to see the correlation between the distribution of sales across the customer categories and the resulting profitability. Just as management would view department level profit and loss information, they will also be able to view how this correlates to the customer tiers.

Some practitioners may wish to consider basing tier segmentations on actual customer profitability (providing it is available) rather than customer spending. While there may be some consideration for this, basing the segments on spending remains the most practical and powerful method to integrate customer data into a company's financial and management reporting. Even in companies with consistent gross profit margins across their product offerings, thus eliminating great differences in customer profit margin, there remain very clear correlations between customer spending and customer value. While in some companies all customers may provide a similar gross profit margin, higher spending customers produce far greater gross profit dollars due to their higher spending, more frequent shopping, and their significantly higher retention over time.

Rather than calculating the customer tier gross profit margins based upon assuming a company gross and then deducting the markdown expense, companies possessing accurate item level cost information will have actual customer tier profitability. While such accuracy is much sought after, the majority of companies must calculate customer profitability as we have in this example, providing close enough approximation for our purposes.

My experience has shown that to be of most value to a company, such tier segmentations should be skewed to the higher end of the spending spectrum observed in a retailer's customer data. Some practitioners are concerned with attempting to create segments that result in tiers having similar numbers of customers. It is much better to skew the segments so as to show far more detail at the higher end of the spending range, for it is here that small increases in pure customer numbers can have an exaggerated effect on profitability.

For example, let's assume a retail company looks at customer spending data for a quarter and finds that its customers have spent from $0.01 up to $1,000.00. If the retailer wished to create a tier segment structure having 5 tiers, he or she would be best to skew the segments to the high end of the spending range. For example:

Tier 1:	$900.00 –	$1,000.00
Tier 2:	$800.00 –	$899.99
Tier 3:	$500.00 –	$799.99
Tier 4:	$300.00 –	$499.99
Tier 5:	< $299.00	

Such a segment scheme would allow the company to observe changes in the composition of the top several tiers over time. Because these highest spending customers generate such strong profit margins, their impact on the company's overall profitability is exaggerated compared to their household numbers. Retailers cognizant of this value skewing in their customer base can leverage minute changes for great impact. Even small increases in the number of customers at the highest tiers can result in far greater profits for the company.

The Power of Benchmarking

Customer Tier reporting provides us a way to measure the impact of marketing (and other things) on customer shopping behavior. The strength of customer tier reporting is magnified by its use as a benchmarking tool, essentially creating a scorecard allowing the company to view changes in its customer base, and the resulting impact upon profitability, over time. In the following example (Report 3-3), we can see how a retailer was able to strongly impact the composition of their customer base over the years by maintaining a strong focus on recognizing and rewarding their higher spending customers.

Quarterly Customer Tier Summary

Customer Tier		Tier 1	Tier 2	Tier 3	Tier 4	Total
% of Households						
	Year 1 / Q1	1.66%	10.29%	14.32%	73.73%	100%
	Year 2 / Q1	2.29%	10.71%	15.09%	71.91%	100%
	Year 3 / Q1	3.06%	10.68%	14.75%	71.51%	100%
	Year 4 / Q1	3.21%	8.98%	13.12%	74.69%	100%
	Year 5 / Q1	3.44%	9.90%	13.48%	73.18%	100%
% of Total Spending						
	Year 1 / Q1	10.32%	36.11%	26.14%	27.43%	100%
	Year 2 / Q1	13.65%	35.47%	25.75%	25.13%	100%
	Year 3 / Q1	18.15%	34.33%	24.07%	23.45%	100%
	Year 4 / Q1	20.38%	31.42%	23.16%	25.04%	100%
	Year 5 / Q1	21.54%	32.48%	22.55%	23.43%	100%
Frequency (Visits per Week)						
	Year 1 / Q1	3.10	2.19	1.45	0.63	
	Year 2 / Q1	3.22	2.29	1.60	0.67	
	Year 3 / Q1	5.16	2.85	1.80	0.79	
	Year 4 / Q1	4.56	2.73	1.72	0.72	
	Year 5 / Q1	4.58	2.64	1.62	0.66	

To explain Report 3-3, in Year 1 we see that Tier 1 households made up only 1.66% of this retailer's total customer households. By Year 5, Tier 1 households made up 3.44% of the company's customer base, more than doubling the number of customers at this highest spending level. We can see the corresponding increase in sales; Tier 1 customers generating only 10.32% of total company sales in Year 1, growing to 21.54% of total sales in Year 2.

Note the increase in shopping frequency, particularly amongst Tier 1 and 2 customers, as the retailer focuses on these customer levels. As mentioned earlier in the book, there is a strong correlation between spending and shopping frequency; as a retailer rewards customer spending over time, inevitably shopping frequency increases.

To see the impact of these changes, let's use the customer tier gross profit margins used in Report 3-2 and apply the customer tier sales mix from the above example (Report 3-3). We see that in Year 1, Tier 1 customers provided 10.32% of total sales (from Report 3-3, Year 1) at an effective margin of 33% (from Report 3-2); Tier 4 customers generated 27.43% of total sales at a margin of 18%. By carrying this out for all the customer tiers we see that this would have produced a total gross margin for the company of 25.19% in Year 1 (Report 3-4).

Report 3-4

Customer Tier Yield Management					
	Tier 1	Tier 2	Tier 3	Tier 4	Total
Year 1					
Customer Tier % of Total Spending	10.32%	36.11%	26.14%	27.43%	
Effective Yield Net of Markdown	33%	30%	23%	18%	
Contribution to Total Gross Margin	**3.41%**	**10.83%**	**6.01%**	**4.94%**	**25.19%**
Year 5					
Customer Tier % of Total Spending	21.54%	32.48%	22.55%	23.43%	
Effective Yield Net of Markdown	33%	30%	23%	18%	
Contribution to Total Gross Margin	**7.11%**	**9.74%**	**5.19%**	**4.22%**	**26.26%**

Increase in total Gross Profit Margin of 1.07% (25.19% to 26.26%) due to change in sales mix; more sales from higher yielding Tier 1 customers, less sales from lower yielding customers.

Duplicating this procedure for Year 5, we see that the total company gross margin has increased to 26.26% simply by changing the composition of the sales base. This company would have increased their total gross profit margin over 1% through practicing customer tier yield management.

In actuality, the improvement in the total company margin would be much greater (the actual gain in this retailer's gross profit margin was in excess of 4%). In the sample reports we are using an assumed gross margin for all customer tiers; in actual practice, the profit margin generated by Tier 1 customers is significantly higher than Tier 4 customers in many retail sectors due to vast differences in the purchasing mix. Tier 1 customers tend to purchase more products at full retail price; lower spending customers tend to be more deal-driven, purchasing more products on sale, thus generating substantially lower margins.

Improvements in customer retention, particularly amongst higher value customers, serve to compound these gains over time. Not only do higher spending customers provide a higher yield, but as the retailer can significantly improve retention of Tier 1 and Tier 2 customers over time, this effect is magnified; more and more value is realized from these customers when viewing their behavior and financial information over years of time.

To maximize gains such as these, retail companies must become disciplined in their marketing expenditures, particularly related to customer-focused marketing. Companies that truly redirect some portion of their total marketing expenditures to fund initiatives intended to change customer shopping realize a much greater bottom line profit gain than those companies incrementally adding the costs of such efforts to their overall marketing expenditures.

The Customer Lifecycle

In past work I have presented the concept of the customer lifecycle, graphically represented below. This attempts to visually present the flow of customers through retail companies; new customers flowing into the company's stores and some going on to become regular customers. Regular customers remain with the company for some period of time, their spending increasing and decreasing as they move through their lifecycle; some regular customers decrease their spending while in the process of departing the company, perhaps for new competitors.

The Customer Lifecycle

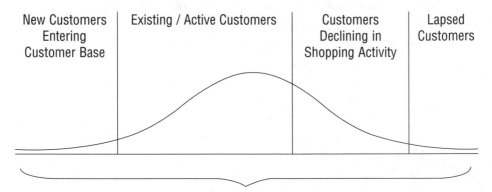

Retailer's Customer Base

It is possible to segment customers into the groups represented in the customer lifecycle figure. New customers would be those customers appearing for the first time in the retailer's stores (for example, those customers applying for a loyalty card). Existing customers can be segmented using the tier segmentation method described previously. Declining customers would be those that were previously at, for example, Tier 1 or Tier 2 and have descended one or two levels. Lapsed customers are those customers who had been active but have not been in the stores for more than three periods (again, the exact definition of a lapsed customer, or any of these, should be that most appropriate for the retailer).

The Customer Lifecycle

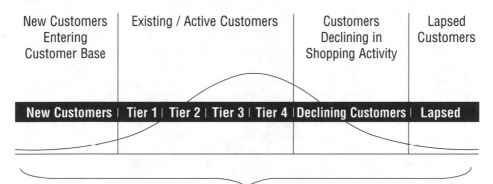

Retailer's Customer Base

Customer Inventory
Total Customer Households Shopping with Retailer

We can bring this view of the ebb and flow of customers through our stores to life by using customer data to numerically represent these concepts. Armed with enough customer data over time, retailers can report customer "inventory", measuring the number of new, existing, declining, reactivated, and lapsed customers in their business. An example is shown in Report 3-5, drawn from an actual retail chain.

		Customer Inventory							
Financial Period	Total Customers	New Customers	Tier 1	Tier 2	Tier 3	Tier 4	Declining Customers	*Reactivated Customers*	Lapsed Customers
3	**137,748** 100%	32,515 24%	4,132 3%	17,907 13%	22,182 16%	44,280 32%	3,746 3%	12,986 9%	53,126
4	**156,305** 100%	35,232 23%	3,126 2%	18,423 12%	28,135 18%	46,892 30%	3,282 2%	21,215 14%	30,141
5	**162,905** 100%	34,259 21%	4,887 3%	17,553 11%	27,694 17%	53,759 33%	3,098 2%	21,655 13%	32,895
6	**161,358** 100%	30,237 19%	3,227 2%	16,136 10%	33,885 20%	53,890 34%	3,812 2%	20,171 13%	37,784
7	**163,770** 100%	29,548 18%	6,551 4%	21,290 12%	35,165 22%	45,856 28%	4,733 3%	20,627 13%	45,083

Definitions:

Total Customers: *The total number of customers shopping during the period (New + Existing+Declining + Reactivated).*

New Customers: *Those customers new to the retailer; first time shoppers identified through loyalty platform.*

Existing / Active Customers: *Those customers who have been active customers during prior periods and continue to shop. Those customers segmented using a Customer Tier segmentation based upon spending thresholds.*

Declining Customers: *Previously Tier 1-2 Customers who have declined to Tier 3-4 Spending.*

Re-activated Customers: *Those customers who had not shopped during 3 prior periods but who have now re-appeared.*

Lapsed Customers: *Customers that have shopped in the past but have not shopped during past 3 periods.*

Through studying this report, and having knowledge of operations, marketing, and normal customer shopping behavior, we can see several items of note.

In Period 3, we can see that there is a large customer group that has lapsed in their shopping; far larger than any subsequent period. This retailer is characterized (as many are) by having a large number of customers shop their stores at the holiday time, only to vanish until the following year. This is evident here; a large number of customers would have shopped in Period 13 (not shown; example is using 13-4 week periods for the year), only to show up in the lifecycle-based customer inventory report as lapsed. Perhaps these customers represent an opportunity for this company; is it possible to create a marketing program to bring them back prior to the next holiday?

In Periods 3 through 5 we see the impact of a marketing initiative to drive new customers into the retailer's stores. The results are evident by measuring the inflow of new customers each period.

Periods 6 and 7 show an increase in the number of customers declining in their shopping. Declining households in this example are those customers who had previously been at Tier 1 or Tier 2 based upon their spending but have declined more than two tier levels. Essentially, these are assets at risk; valuable customers who are decreasing their spending (and probably shopping visits) with the company, possibly on their way to defecting entirely. From a marketing perspective, these customers represent a strong opportunity for investment.

Certainly this information can be extended to report such measures as results versus budget and/or the prior year, and year-to-date figures for total company and same store average results. Using measures of this type, management can now view the average number of customer households per store and compare to budget or prior year measures to learn if the customer base is growing or shrinking.

Customer Retention

So as to further capitalize on these relationships, we must append customer retention measures to reporting. While some leading companies view their customer retention rates on a rolling weekly basis, others measure retention each financial period or each quarter. Whatever the basis, the value of customer retention measures lies in viewing trends over time, a single retention measure providing only a snapshot view of activity.

Customer retention measures can be structured in many ways, some more suited to particular retail channels than others. Following is a framework for further consideration:

 Overall customer retention measures:
- All customers year to year (for example, of all customers shopping in Q1 last year, how many remain active in Q1 this year?).
- Measure by customer tier, (for example, of all customers in Tier 1 last year, how many have been retained overall? The number retained as Tier 1 this year? The number dropping to Tier 2, and so on.).

➤ Customer retention by lifecycle:
  - New customers: of new customers joining in Q1 last year, how many were retained through Q1 this year? How many new customers were retained three months after joining (a typical falling off point)? How do the rates compare with activity in the present year?
  - Declining customer retention: of those customers classified as declining during the same period the prior year, how many are still with the company? How does the rate compare to activity this year? What is the retention of declining customers period to period?

➤ Long term customer retention: of those customers active in the first year of the company's program, how many are still active in Year 2? How many increased their spending? How many decreased in spending? Stayed the same? Of those Year 1 customers active in Year 2, how many were retained through Year 3? And so on, the process then repeated for each year.

This last area, measuring the retention of customers over years of time, is one of great opportunity. In researching those customers retained by retail companies over years, we see that their value when measured against the performance of other transitory consumers continually grows over time. For companies having access to multiple years' worth of customer data, the first goal would be to glean the relative handful of customer households shopping over the long period and actively working to recognize and retain them into the future. The company can then add customers each year to their Long Term Best Customer group as they surface from the data.

Using customer-based reporting, retail companies can now create the link between marketing and the company's financial position.

Financial Results

Customer Tier Analysis
Customer Inventory
Customer Retention

Marketing

While marketing people can find enormous wealth in customer databases, at the end of the day the final evaluation of effectiveness is this: Have the actions of marketing assisted in increasing the number of customers shopping with the business, increased retention of customers - particularly high value customers, improved spending of existing customers, and increased the value of the customer base? These are now the metrics that retail executives can be, and are, including in their regular management reporting, drawing a clear connection between a firm's marketing and advertising tactics and customer performance. Retailers can now see the customers behind the sales.

The tools of tier analyses, customer inventory, and retention measures provide the litmus test for any and all marketing, merchandising, and operational initiatives. Retailers possessing detailed knowledge of their customers, and properly structuring the data, can now clearly measure the effects upon sales, profitability, customer retention, and customer yield. Structuring customer data in these ways also helps propagate the understanding and use of customer knowledge throughout a retailer's operations.

CUSTOMER FOCUSED MARKETING

Part One: Marketing via the Customer Lifecycle

Retailers enlightened to the differences in value between their customers, and understanding the lifecycle stages related to customer behavior, can begin to articulate marketing strategies and tactics to particular segments in order to maximize performance and improve the return on investment of their marketing expenditures.

Though there may be some overlap with more traditional loyalty marketing and the practice of best customer marketing, the ability to view customers through the lens of lifecycle stages and tier analysis provides far greater potential to focus marketing efforts and measure effectiveness.

In more channels than not, retailers have historically gone to market with customer incentives that in actuality promote customer promiscuity, the opposite behavior that most retail companies truly seek. Advertising circulars promoting commodity items at low prices convince customers that the best way to maximize their spending is to shop at competing retailers, purchasing the sale items at each. Magazine companies are one of the worst culprits of this type of behavior. By letting magazine subscriptions lapse, the publisher will send increasingly valuable offers trying to entice the "lost customer" back. The magazine's regular readers pay full fare; the customers who have deserted the company get the best prices. In essence, magazine companies are rewarding customer defection, providing the best prices to lapsed customers and in the process penalizing their existing, full fare subscribers.

Most cellular telephone companies are another excellent example of this schizophrenic marketing. Rather than reward continuity of service, many cellular service providers are constantly promoting ever-lower prices and more minutes of service, many of them having up to 30% or more of their active customer base defecting each year to competing providers.

During the past decade, as retail loyalty marketing has developed, practitioners have tried to move away from these past marketing methods, instead focusing on improving spending and retention of their existing customers. Much of this work has focused on best customer programs; the recognition and reward of a company's most valuable customers. Best customer marketing can be defined as the skewing of benefits to those customers deemed more valuable to the business, or those that have potential of becoming a high value customer. The philosophy behind recognizing and rewarding best customers is one of the bedrock principles of traditional loyalty marketing. The rationale and economic arguments supporting this practice have been well documented by the likes of Frederick Reichheld, in his several works on the value of customer loyalty, and Brian Woolf, in his works specifically related to loyalty marketing in a retail supermarket environment.

It has been proven time and again that it is far easier and more cost effective to encourage those people already good customers of a retailer to do even more shopping with their favored store. These customers are already predisposed to the retailer as evidenced by their shopping behavior. But even though best customers have a favorite store in any given channel, many times they do not think twice about shopping with a competitor out of convenience. For example, the customer that loves her neighborhood supermarket readily stops at the convenience store across the street to purchase milk on the way home for that evening's meal.

Many retail companies possessing some level of customer information have focused a majority of their efforts on recognizing and rewarding their best customers. Some have done this by redirecting some portion of their past marketing expenditures to funding increased values for their best customers, thereby increasing those customers' spending and retention. As a result these companies have experienced gains, in some cases very substantial gains, to their gross profit margins. These gains have come from encouraging the already higher spending customers to do yet more shopping with the retailer (purchasing more products and services at regular price/margin), and from discouraging some of the cherry-pickers, those customers purchasing only deal merchandise.

As they have discouraged some of the deal-seekers, successful practitioners of best customer marketing many times see their transaction counts begin to drop slightly from such deal seekers going elsewhere, but these declines are more than offset by increases in the average transaction size. The end result is fewer customers, but those remaining are spending more and generating a higher margin.

While best customer marketing can produce strong profit gains during the transition of the customer base, the gains tend to level off after an initial surge. A number of retail companies reaching this point wonder where to turn next for growth.

Through customer-focused marketing as we are discussing it here, the retailer is seeking to maximize the performance of their already higher spending customers, but in addition is seeking to improve results from the company's marketing expenditures across the entire customer base. The reports and concepts detailed in the preceding chapter, specifically the customer inventory report and customer tier profit and loss statement, provide the company the management tools necessary to allocate marketing expenditures for the best return.

Customer-Focused Marketing

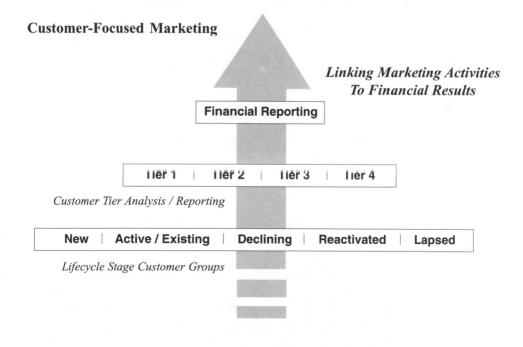

Financial Reporting

Linking Marketing Activities To Financial Results

| Tier 1 | Tier 2 | Tier 3 | Tier 4 |

Customer Tier Analysis / Reporting

| New | Active / Existing | Declining | Reactivated | Lapsed |

Lifecycle Stage Customer Groups

Leading companies are now able to target their marketing efforts at these separate customer segments, knowing that the opportunity to maximize performance within each of these customer groups requires a mix of different messages, values, information, and so on. For example, a retailer should wish to nurture new customers, informing them of special reasons for returning to the store and perhaps providing an incentive to do so. Conversely, the message to a best customer should convey the importance of the customer to the company with the goals of fostering the relationship and increasing retention of the customer.

What follows is not so much a litany of specific marketing programs as a framework for retail companies to think within. The framework provided by tier reporting and the customer inventory can provide the structure for measuring the results of marketing initiatives while giving marketers free reign in developing their own unique tactical executions.

Targeting Customer Lifecycle Stages

Using the customer lifecycle concept, we can categorize customers into one of five groupings: new customers, existing / active customers, declining customers, reactivated customers, and those customers that have lapsed. Strategies and tactics can be developed targeting each of these customer segments so as to increase the efficacy of retail marketing.

New Customers...

Retail mass marketing activities can be distilled to two primary efforts: the first is building and positioning the retailer relative to competitors (brand image), the other is to attract customers to the stores. Marketing then communicates information needed to accomplish these goals, such as conveying product assortment or quality, or special pricing to encourage consumers to visit the company's stores. Ad flyers, commonly used by many retail sectors, are sometimes justified as providing values to existing customers (special pricing, etc.), but at their core the purpose of ad flyers is to bring consumers to the door.

In this sense, we can see the role of mass marketing in attracting new customers. But by using customer-based measures of new customer shopping behavior, and by drawing upon the experience of some retail companies that have discontinued a large part of their traditional mass (price-based) marketing, we can see other areas of opportunity.

A small number of retailers around the world have, for some extended period of time, discontinued their usual ad flyers or price-based advertising. These companies found that this has had little effect on the inflow of new customers to their stores; rather, each has found, the opportunity lies in working to better retain those customers already coming in the door as new. Several years ago, Lisa Piron of Green Hills focused on new customer behavior at the store and discovered some alarming statistics.

Green Hills observed that approximately 50% of new customers visiting the store for the first time failed to return for a second visit; that is half of all new customers never returned to the store. Further, of the 50% of new customers that did return, half of them disappeared within one to two more visits. Green Hills found it was retaining only 25%-30% of all new customers over time.

Customer-Focused Marketing
New Customers

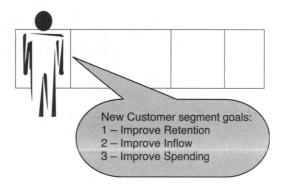

Before the reader assumes that this is aberrant consumer behavior, consider this: we have found similar patterns at supermarket retailers across the United States, be they independent grocers or large chains. Moreover, I have found similar relationships at supermarkets and hypermarkets in Europe and Asia. In many retail sectors, companies would be better served to concentrate their efforts at retaining new customers once in their doors, rather than spending mass sums of money to attract new consumers each week.

Changing customers' shopping habits is very difficult to do, especially for retail sectors exhibiting high shopping frequency such as convenience stores or supermarkets. Consumers tend to become comfortable with a store they regularly visit, knowing where products are located, idiosyncrasies of the store's checkout process, and so on. Many retailers are guilty of assumption; assuming all customers (even new ones) know what hours the store is open, where everything is in the store, and what credit cards are accepted.

Astute retailers understand that to retain a new customer they must immediately begin educating the new customer about the store and reinforcing the customer visiting the store again. Some companies provide new customers a brochure or other material informing them of the store's hours, payment methods, services, and perhaps the names and telephone of the store's management team. Other retailers have gone further, encouraging repeat visits by offering the new customer a gift certificate of some value in return for the customer's spending a certain amount within a period of weeks. Yet other companies send a direct mail piece to the new customer each week for the first several weeks so as to keep their name in front of the customer, explaining some of the unique services or signature products the store offers, and so on.

It is strongly suggested that a company not concentrate on trying to dial up the inflow of new customers until effective new customer retention programs, and proper measurements, are in place.

Piron's discovery at Green Hills led the retailer to develop a new customer marketing effort aimed at improving the retention of people shopping with the store for the first time. This effort took the form of developing a small brochure given to new customers explaining the history of the store, services offered, hours open, and so on. In addition, it explained why Green Hills was different from its chain store competitors. New customers were provided two different offers, one encouraging them to spend that day and entitling them to a discount for spending at higher levels, and a second offer entitling the customer to a $30 gift certificate for spending $300 during the next six weeks.

Direct mail was also used to contact the new customer over the next several weeks, again informing them of reasons for shopping with Green Hills and enclosing offers for samples of signature products.

Through such efforts, Green Hills was able to increase retention of new customers, on average, by over 10% from levels prior to focusing on this segment.

Existing / Active Customers...

This group of customers predictably accounts for a majority of the customer base of most any retailer. The customer tier reporting tool and retention measures provide the benchmarking necessary for companies to evaluate their efforts related to retaining these customers over time and encouraging them to do more shopping with the retailer.

Customer value is derived from the aggregation of the customer's spending, shopping frequency, mix of products or services purchased, and the customer's shopping behavior over time; measured as customer retention. Which factors a retailer should attempt to impact favorably upon, and in which order, is dependent upon several variables.

Customer Value Derived From 4 Factors...

$ Average Spend per Visit
X   Frequency of Shopping
X   Gross Profit Margin of Products Purchase
X   Time
_____
=   **Customer Values**

Consumers purchase food to consume at home on a frequent basis, but even so the typical consumer may visit a supermarket only once a week, filling the gaps with stops at the convenience store or other stores now selling food Many supermarkets have had great success influencing customer shopping behavior by altering the reward structure offered to consumers; rewarding the consumer for their spending over time. Thus, the supermarket has created a disincentive for the consumer to visit the convenience store.

At one time, Rice Epicurean Markets of Houston, Texas, offered their customers the ability to collect airline miles based upon their purchasing. During one promotion, customers were encouraged to spend more than they had on average in the past in return for double miles. The result was an impressive 50% increase in spending during the promotion by those households that participated. While some portion of these additional sales may have come from increased consumption, most of the sales gain came out of competitors' pockets.

Other retailers have had success encouraging their customers to shop more frequently, knowing that spending will also increase as customers visit the store more often. There is some debate over which comes first; does spending follow frequency or is increased shopping frequency a result of rewarding spending? Many retailers have found that by recognizing and rewarding customers' spending, an increase in shopping frequency naturally follows.

Customer-Focused Marketing
Existing / Active Customers

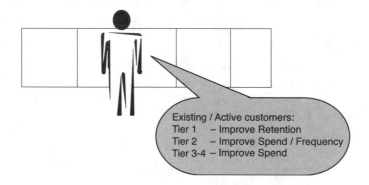

Existing / Active customers:
Tier 1 – Improve Retention
Tier 2 – Improve Spend / Frequency
Tier 3-4 – Improve Spend

Typically, retailers experience a substantial gain to their gross profit margins as they encourage customers to shop more frequently and spend more. By rewarding shopping behavior over time, customers now have incentive to purchase more products offered at regular price in addition to purchasing products in departments and categories previously ignored.

The last primary area of shopping behavior retailers can capitalize on is customer retention; maintaining a customer over a longer period of time. There are huge differences in value amongst a retailer's customers. Knowing this, leading companies now focus their efforts on retaining the most valuable customers over time.

While spending is perhaps the easiest variable to quickly affect, retailers pursuing this tactic must be careful in practice. Depending upon the pricing and marketing philosophy of a given retailer, all sales dollars will not necessarily offer the same level of profitability. Some retail companies maintain relative consistency across their product or service offerings, most all products generating a similar level of gross profit margin. Other retailers, such as those going to market with a high-low pricing philosophy, can have vast differences in the profit margin offered by their different products. Supermarket companies are a prime example of this, selling some products (front page loss leaders) at a pure loss in the hope of generating customer traffic, while other products in the store provide high levels of margin.

In the case of retailers able to maintain a consistent margin across their product offering, any increase in customer spending equates to an increase in gross profit margin dollars. This correlation does not necessarily hold true for a promotional department store where a customer can spend a great deal of money but generate a very low, sometimes even negative, gross margin if purchasing only products offered at deal prices.

On average, if customers increase their spending with a company, they also provide a larger profit margin. Many retailers can realize substantial gains by focusing on this one attribute of customer behavior. But, as the number of retail loyalty programs has increased, customer savvy has also grown. In a number of markets it is not unusual to see several competing retailers each operating a loyalty program, and each going to market with programs designed to reward customer spending behavior. Some consumers have evolved into a higher form of the well known cherry-picker: customers shopping with a store to earn the promised rewards but purchasing only the deal merchandise offered at low price (and margin), then moving on to the next retailer to do the same.

We can find an analogy to this type of purchasing behavior in the airline industry. Some flyers earn their frequent flyer designations and benefits by purchasing full fare tickets; other flyers always buy heavily discounted fares, yet are able to earn the same benefits. The first type of customers are highly profitable for the airline, the second group much less so. It is to address this situation that companies such as American Airlines have developed the systems that allow them to now measure the profitability of their customers.

Based upon each customer's value rating, customized offers and rewards are then communicated.[2]

While this consumer behavior in the retail world is not necessarily the norm, it is something to be on guard for. This is an important reason driving advanced practitioners to measure customer profitability.

Declining Customers...

Some companies have done fascinating work involving customers who are declining in their shopping behavior (either spending less and/or shopping less frequently), attempting to retain these customers prior to their becoming lapsed. Rice Epicurean Markets is one of these leading edge retailers.

Customer-Focused Marketing
Declining Customers

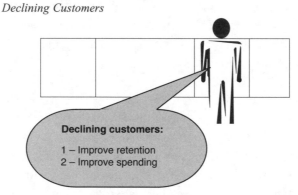

On one occasion, Rice Epicurean identified Tier 1 customers that had slipped to Tier 3 or below. Designing a set of offers and incentives, Rice mailed the package off to the declining customers that had been identified. An impressive 46% of the targeted customers responded to the incentives, boosting their spending considerably and maintaining a much higher level than that they had declined to.

Experience has shown that these types of efforts, directed at customers who are in the declining phase of shopping, pay much better dividends than attempting to bring back customers once they have lapsed entirely. While it is possible to lure most anyone back after his or her defection with rich enough incentives, the challenge is to bring such customers back regularly without the costly enticements.

Reactivated Customers...

Some retail companies wish to include the category of Reactivated Customers in their customer inventories. These are customers that were previously lapsed but have reappeared in the store.

This is a relatively new area for customer intelligent retail companies to be working in, but one that shows promise. Most work being done at present revolves about attempting to learn what brought these customers back into the stores. Was it a certain ad flyer, or perhaps a featured product or mix of products?

For example, one retail company runs a special sale event twice a year. This company is in the process of evaluating the impact of these sales on the reactivated customer segment, seeking to learn if this one event brings back these otherwise lost customers, or does the event cater more to the regular customers?

Lapsed Customers...

When considering the possibilities presented by having a great deal of customer information, many retailers, looking for that "silver bullet" sales increase, leap to the idea of winning back lapsed customers, those customers that have stopped shopping with the store altogether.

Customer-Focused Marketing
Lapsed Customers

Lapsed customers:
1 – Learn why they left
2 – Attempt to bring back
(concentrate on high value lapsed customers)

While this seems to be a popular thought amongst retailers, actual experience has taught us caution. Many companies have experimented with lost customer programs, attempting to win back shoppers that have left the company to shop elsewhere. By making offers rich enough it is possible to pull some lost shoppers back. The challenge lies in keeping those lost customers coming back without the heavy incentives.

There is perhaps a better course to take with these customers. First and foremost, any company attempting to do any work in this area would be wise to confine their focus to only formerly high value customers who have stopped shopping. It does not make much sense to spend any substantial sum of money attempting to bring back a customer who was not profitable to begin with.

Some retail companies have had success with viewing their high value lapsed customers as a learning opportunity, attempting to correspond with the lapsed customer to find out why they left; an exit interview if you will. In this way the retailer is able to sometimes identify operational or product quality problems that can be addressed in hopes of preventing future loss of customers. This type of education can serve as an early warning system, alerting the company to problems they may not have known existed.

How could this work in the real world of retail? Let's look at the experience of Gap, Inc. during the late 1990s and into 2001.

During 2000 and 2001, Gap experienced dramatic business declines after having rapidly expanded the number of stores it operated. Same store sales were dropping at double-digit rates and its stock price had declined precipitously. During this time, the Gap had moved away from its core fashion focus, offering instead trendier clothing which did not appeal to its primary customer base.

If the Gap had been capturing and using detailed customer information, management of the company may have had clear evidence that severe problems were coming. Prior to any serious decline in sales figures, the shopping frequency and the average transaction size amongst its Tier 1 customers would have most likely started showing evidence of deterioration. Further, had the company been regularly measuring the retention of its different customer segments, it would have noticed an accelerating trend in declining customer retention, its higher value clientele of most concern.

By conducting market research, focus groups, and exit surveys amongst the recently lapsed good customers, the company may have learned that its new fashion offerings were not appealing to its core customer.

In some cases, as a result of contacting the lapsed customer and expressing concern over why they left, it is possible to win them back to becoming a regular shopper once again. This can be a positive byproduct of the exit interview process.

The Effectiveness of Mass Marketing

Most all retail companies make use of mass marketing and advertising vehicles such as ad flyers, radio, television, etc. By taking advantage of customer-based measures, companies can work to evaluate the effectiveness and role of these costly endeavors.

Mass Marketing Evaluation

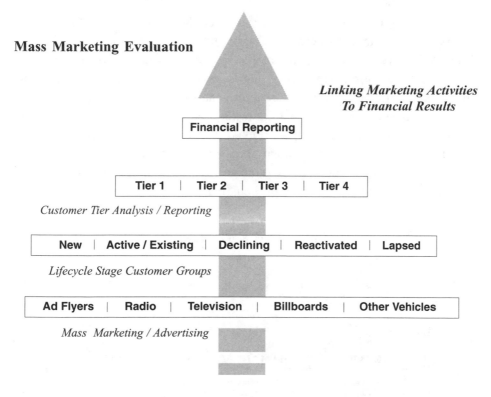

Linking Marketing Activities
To Financial Results

Financial Reporting

| Tier 1 | Tier 2 | Tier 3 | Tier 4 |

Customer Tier Analysis / Reporting

| New | Active / Existing | Declining | Reactivated | Lapsed |

Lifecycle Stage Customer Groups

| Ad Flyers | Radio | Television | Billboards | Other Vehicles |

Mass Marketing / Advertising

One of the largest marketing expenditures for many retailers is their ad flyers. It is not uncommon for companies to produce thousands, even millions, of flyers on a weekly basis; many times the distribution of the flyers is even more costly than the actual production. Depending upon the locale, ad flyers can be distributed by postal code areas or carrier routes. Some companies make use of direct delivery services such as those provided by ADVO and similar businesses; regardless of the specifics, almost all retailers have the ability to distribute flyers based upon some method providing for distribution in some areas and not others.

By creating a matrix overlaying customer lifecycle stage groupings onto the number of flyers distributed by postal code (or whatever scheme), one can explore the effect of this form of marketing. Analysis such as this is best done when viewing a longer period of time, for example a quarter or even a year; because of the nature of customer shopping behavior, this type of analysis can be ineffectual or even misleading when done on tighter time frames.

As we can see in the following report, this retail company is able to view, by postal code, the number of customers brought to the store as a result of the ad flyer. While we are not able to make a definitive correlation between the ad flyer and the customer appearing in the store, we will assume that if the customer does shop with the retailer, that the flyer was not wasted. Furthermore, we can measure the shrink related to ad flyer distribution; measuring the number of flyers distributed in an area that were wasted, i.e. did not result in the customer shopping. By appending a cost (including production and distribution costs) to the shrink, the retailer is able to measure the economic waste associated with their flyers.

Ad Flyer Distribution	Total Distributed	Total Cost	Existing / Active Customers							Effective Total	Shrink	
			New	Tier 1	Tier 2	Tier 3	Tier 4	Declining	Reactivated		#	$
Postal Code 1	2,056	$20,313.28	14	232	254	311	217	35	26	1,089	967	$9,553.96
Postal Code 2	1,578	$15,590.64	27	506	376	369	155	28	43	1,504	74	$731.12
Postal Code 3	3,893	$38,462.84	53	138	266	471	426	19	67	1,440	2,453	$24,235.64
Postal Code 4 ...etc.	2,404	$23,751.52	17	5	8	23	27	2	5	87	2,317	$22,891.96
Total	9,931	$98,118.28	111	881	904	1,174	825	84	141	4,120	5,811	$57,412.68

N.B. Total cost and shrink calculated using $0.19 as cost of flyer x 52 week distribution.
N.B. The figures used are from an actual retail company based upon 12 months activity.

A further analysis would involve stating the sales and gross profit from each of the Postal Code areas by customer segment and then deducting the ad flyer distribution expense, measuring the return in each area.

Customer intelligent retailers can utilize this information for developing their marketing plans, such as deciding new areas to target for customer development. The retailer used in this example has identified Postal Code area 4 as one for development. Their efforts to attract customers from this area are in the early stages, but the company is making use of this type data to assist in evaluation of their effectiveness.

In addition, we can see that 58% of the expense related to distributing ad flyers in these postal codes is wasted (shrink of $57,412 on total expenditure of $96,118). To reiterate: the distribution of nearly 10,000 ad flyers each week over a year's time into these postal codes results in only 4,000 customers shopping with the store during the year. This example is not an anomaly; similar results may be found when studying most any retail company's ad flyer distribution and corresponding customer behavior. No wonder customer intelligent retailers are working so hard to develop more advanced communications with their customers.

Customer Metric Solutions is a company bringing together customer data and traditional retail sales information and combining it with census and demographic data and mapping tools. The company's CustomerINSITE tool provides a geographic view of customer data, enabling retail companies to view the trade area around their stores and can profile customers or prospects within the trading area. By linking this information with media costs, retail companies can make more intelligent and informed decisions as to how they spend their mass marketing dollars.

While most are not this advanced, a number of retail companies are making use of this type analysis to help rationalize their ad flyer expenditures. By evaluating the returns from each area of distribution, these companies make decisions as to maintain distribution or to terminate it, perhaps instead mailing the ad flyer to the handful of valuable customers within an area dropped. In even the largest retail companies using ad flyers and possessing some level of customer data, we have found extensive opportunity for cost savings without jeopardizing sales.

A similar methodology can be applied to other factors relevant to ad flyers. A few advanced practitioners evaluate the actual items and products featured in their flyers using a similar matrix. Analysis would include stating both actual sales and unit movement by each customer group. An added benefit to viewing this analysis by units sold is that clear indications begin to appear as to which specific products may (or may not) appeal to the different customer groups, the idea being to work towards featuring products that appeal most to the more valuable customers and/or are proven effective at attracting new customers or reactivating lapsed customers.

Retail companies can also learn of the importance of specific price points related to flyer items and the accompanying markdown expense. By tracking products sold at different price points during different periods, retailers can begin to learn how strong a correlation may exist between certain prices on specific products and customer appeal. Related to this is the measurement of markdown expense across the customer groups, perhaps learning if this expenditure can be used to greater effect in some areas more than others.

This type of analysis begins to directly link merchandising with marketing to improve the efficiencies of both in working to improve customer performance. A reverse of this methodology can be used in determining which of the company's product categories or sections may have most appeal to the different customer groups, enabling the company to understand which categories or products to feature in order to attract the desired customers.

While offering much less conclusive and delineated information, companies can also use this type analysis to help determine the effectiveness of other forms of mass marketing and advertising such as radio, television, billboards, and so on. For example, if a retailer runs a television campaign for a given month, the company could view the customer activity (both in terms of numbers of customers shopping within each group and their accompanying sales) for the period, thereby comparing it to the same period the year prior and the periods preceding and subsequent to the campaign. While it is impossible to isolate the impact of these marketing activities in companies making use of both at the same time, the added information provided by viewing customer activity provides that much more data with which to improve decision making.

As much as possible, companies will wish to link their mass marketing activities to results as evidenced by shopping behavior viewed through the lens of lifecycle stage customer segments and, ultimately, financial-based customer tier reporting.

Customer-Focused Marketing – the long term view

The element of time must be brought into the retail marketing equation. Based on evidence accumulated by a handful of leading companies we know that some customers are likely to shop with a retailer for a number of years. With this in mind, we must consider changing our marketing strategies and tactics to seize upon the knowledge.

Historically, many retail companies have implemented marketing programs that are "fixed" in the sense that they are based upon customers purchasing certain products or product categories. Retail companies tend to view the world through the lens of product information.

Traditional Marketing Programs

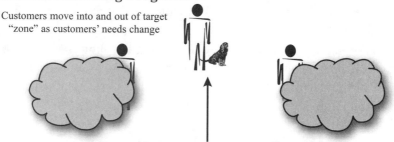

Customers move into and out of target "zone" as customers' needs change

Many marketing programs are "fixed" — the customers move into and out of the target zone, the retailer not "seeing" the customer until they come into view.

Carol Customer has shopped at her local supermarket for some time and has been a member of their loyalty program for well over a year. Living alone, Carol has never purchased a great deal of food and has never received any special offers or recognition from her store.

Carol gets a dog and begins purchasing pet food when she shops. Within a month or so Carol receives a letter from the store welcoming her to their pet club, informing her that for every $50 in pet product purchases, she will receive a $5 gift certificate. Carol continues to shop and begins to receive the gift certificates periodically.

Some months later Carol accepts a new position at work in which she must travel a great deal. Realizing the travel will make pet owning difficult, she gives her dog to a friend and stops purchasing pet food. Carol does not hear from her supermarket again.

Traditionally, marketing in the retail industry has been product driven; in the example just given, the promotion revolved about pet food. The store maintains their product focus, waiting until customers appear within their field of view (purchasers of pet products) to acknowledge them with some type of offer.

Consider now that the customer intelligent retail company has the ability to follow a customer as the customer's shopping patterns evolve. This implies a far different view of marketing than retail companies have had in the past.

Carol Customer has shopped with a well-known local department store for some time. Being a regular shopper and a member of the store's valued customer program, Carol often receives special offers and advance notification of when new apparel by designers she likes will be in the store.

The store marketing department notices one day that Carol has made inquiries in the store's bridal shop for her upcoming wedding. Armed with the knowledge that Carol is making a lifestyle change, the store includes offers on items correlating with newlyweds in her mailings.

Carol continues shopping, appreciating the offers and information that the store regularly provides her. A year or so later, the store marketing department notices that Carol is now making purchases from the maternity department; another lifestyle change.

The store tailors their marketing yet again, including offers for maternity wear and information relevant to new parents. Over time, the store tailors the mix of offers, information, and recognition to Carol's new family.

Much information can be gleaned from detailed customer shopping information. Consider that in a department store setting the retailer could identify those customers purchasing maternity wear; this sets the stage for marketing baby needs. Knowing, then, that the customer has children, the retailer can tailor their marketing messages to the customer household as it evolves over time and the children grow. Building a historical record of customer purchasing information can be incredibly powerful.

The ability to capitalize on this knowledge will require new skills and marketing capabilities. As retailers, our ultimate goal can become to build relationships with our individual customers and provide for their needs as they evolve through time.

Customer-driven "Fluid" Marketing

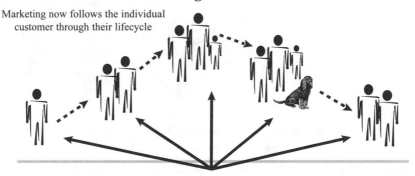

Marketing now follows the individual customer through their lifecycle

Through customer information, retail marketing can now track along with the customer as she evolves, marketing to her needs at different life stages.

Larger retail companies operating multiple formats have the unique capability to capitalize on this concept. While the Gap may have always thought that Gap Kids stores would appeal to Gap customers with children, they could not know for sure without detailed customer information. If the company were to have this data, they could measure the amount of cross-shopping and seek to maximize it.

By changing our marketing perspective, or at least incorporating a new customer perspective, companies can work to tailor their marketing to the customer based upon the customer's needs, acknowledging that the customer's needs may change over time. In this sense marketing needs to become fluid, moving with the customer, not remaining fixed.

The new challenge for customer intelligent retailers is to not only add customer-focused marketing activities to their mix, but to seek the opportune balance between mass marketing activities and customer-focused efforts so as to maximize return on investment of marketing expenditures. While these initiatives can take the form of best customer marketing, companies can make use of the expanded view afforded by customer-based management reporting to evolve beyond this approach.

**The new marketing challenge:
seeking the opportune mix.**

Mass
Marketing

Customer-Focused
Marketing

*What's the right "mix" for building sales, **profitably**?*

Retailers must experiment and decide for themselves the most practical – and profitable – way to structure their customer data for marketing purposes, this structure depending upon the channel and products being sold. For example, in a conventional mass market food retailer, a customer tier structure may be most effective; in stores focusing on natural and organic foods, a lifestyle-based segmentation may be most effective. The key is that regardless of the structure of the data for marketing purposes, each endeavor must now prove itself by the new scorecard: the company profit and loss statement with accompanying customer data.

Part Two: Marketing Driven Customer Segmentation

Working within any of the lifecycle stages can require the use of further customer segmentation. For example, a retailer wishing to improve the shopping or retention of their existing customers is confronted with a large customer population. Further targeting of specific customers can yield improved results and increased return on investment. The possible ways in which a customer base can be segmented go on ad infinitum.

Marketing people the world over have their own preferred methods for segmenting and targeting customers; we will present some of the more widely used methods in the following material. The key point to be made, however, is that marketing departments can use whatever segmentation schemes they prefer, but targeting those methods to the customer lifecycle stage, and evaluating results as measured by the customer inventory, tier analysis, and customer retention, will lead to improved results for the company.

Customer-Focused Marketing

*Linking Marketing Activities
To Financial Results*

Financial Reporting

Tier 1 | Tier 2 | Tier 3 | Tier 4

New | Active / Existing | Declining | Reactivated | Lapsed

Lifestyle groups | RFS Segmentations | Best Customers | Other Marketing Segmentations

Best Customer Segmentations...

How a retailer defines a best customer is dependent upon the depth of the company's customer data and the retailer's sophistication in analyzing and reporting customer shopping behavior. Defining best customers for an operational purpose is typically better served by using a simpler segmentation method; one usually based upon spending within a specified period of time. For example, a best customer can be defined as one who is in the top 20% of customers during a quarter when ranked by spending. Some companies prefer to relate a Best Customer definition to both spending and shopping frequency; for example, defining a Best Customer as someone in the top 20% of customers when ranked by spending or in the top 20% of customers when ranked by frequency, again when viewed over a certain period of time.

A decile-based customer shopping behavior report can easily provide the basis for best customer segmentations. Such a report presents customers based upon their spending, ranking customers from lowest to highest (or vice versa). This basic reporting is easily understood by people throughout the company and provides a straightforward method of segmenting customers.

RFS Segmentations...

RFS stands for Recency, Frequency, and Spending (also sometimes referred to as an RFM segmentation, M standing for Monetary). Customer segmentation involving monetary spending, shopping frequency, and recency of shopping have been mainstays of database marketing for years. These efforts have grown from the direct mail industry; such companies realized years ago that consumers ranking high in any individual attribute (spending, frequency, or recency) would have a much greater propensity for responding to a given offer. These marketers were able to increase the power of this type of segmentation through different combinations of these attributes.

Using this method, retailers first rank their customers by spending; they may use deciles, quintiles, quartiles, or any other appropriate grouping. They next rank their customers based upon recency of shopping using the same ranking method. Lastly, the retailer segments their customers by frequency of shopping. When complete, the marketer has a table that looks akin to the one below.

R-F-S Segmentation			
	Spending	Recency	Frequency
Top 30% of Customers	S1	R1	F1
Middle 40% of Customers	S2	R2	F2
Bottom 30% of Customers	S3	R3	F3

Marketers using this tool have found that customers in the top ranking of any of the individual attributes are most likely to respond to an offer, those customers having a higher redemption rate of offers proffered them. Going further, marketers have found that they can further increase their marketing return on investment by combining different segments; for example, making an offer to any customer residing in R1 S1 F1, or R2 S1 F2, and so on.

RFS segmentations are a powerful force when used as a marketing tool. Retailers can use such segmentations or combinations of such segmentations for use in defining Best Customers. For example, a retailer may decide to classify a consumer as a best customer if they are in the top 30% of customers when ranked by spending, OR if they are in the top 30% of customers when ranked by frequency, OR if they have shopped recently. Analysts or marketers conversant in Boolean logic can segment a customer base using various combinations of shopping attributes in order to accomplish any number of objectives.

As has been shown in the direct mail and catalog industries, this type of segmentation can be appropriate for retailers wishing to present some offer or set of offers to their more valuable, or most likely to respond, customers. For example, many retailers partner with vendors to make an offer for a specific product to some portion of the retailer's customer base; e.g., $1 off any gallon size of brand X laundry detergent. The retailer, attempting to reach the group of customers most likely to respond, may send the offer to customers that are within the top 30% of laundry detergent customers when ranked by spending, OR in the top 30% of laundry detergent customers when ranked by purchasing frequency, OR in the top 30% of customers ranked by recency of shopping.

While an RFS segmentation scheme can be effective with regard to certain marketing endeavors, it presents challenges when used to define best customers for operational purposes. How will a front line employee respond when asked by a consumer what they have to do to receive a certain best customer privilege or service? Educating front line staff in Boolean logic arguments and recency, frequency, and spending may encompass a larger challenge than many wish to undertake.

Lifestyle Segmentations

Retailers rich in customer data, and having diversity in their product sets, may wish to employ marketing segmentations based upon lifestyle groupings. Simple examples would include a supermarket company creating lifestyle groupings based upon products such as natural and organic foods, pet foods, etc.

This type marketing is transferable to a number of other sectors. Bookstores can easily make use of lifestyle segmentations for marketing purposes. Earlier in the book we mentioned that Borders was pursuing a category management structure; this readily lends itself to supporting lifestyle or category-based customer segmentations for marketing purposes. In the department store channel this could include segments built around designer labels, sportswear versus evening wear, and so on.

Related to lifestyle-based segmentation is the practice of some companies in which they append psycho-demographic information to their customer data, making use of this additional information in their analysis. Several large database companies make such information available (at a price) which can be readily imported into a database, married to existing information.

Marketers may wish to focus on customers meeting certain demographic attributes (household size, income, etc.), or that fit within certain psycho-graphic parameters (preference for luxury items, travel, etc.).

Use of this information can be incorporated into the new customer marketing process. For example, the retail company that, having developed the ideal customer demographic, purchases a mailing list of prospects within range of their store that meet the criteria. The store then invites these prospects to start shopping with the store and join the company's loyalty program.

Tier Segmentations....

The power of the customer tier management tool can be strengthened by viewing the structure through two different perspectives: segmentation done for financial purposes, and segmentation done for marketing purposes. Segmentation for financial management reporting has already been described in detail i.e. using specific spending thresholds in certain time periods to create the tiers. The tier concept can be adapted for marketing purposes by applying the concept of time and using Boolean logic arguments.

As discussed, one can define customer loyalty in a number of ways. It can be expressed in terms of pure spending, or in terms of purchasing frequency, or perhaps even in terms of how long a customer has shopped with a retailer. There is validity in each of these measures, but perhaps they offer even more weight if we combine them.

At Green Hills, the definition of customer loyalty was debated for some time. While the management team was very comfortable with the pure spending-based customer segmentation used in their financial reporting, management was not quite as comfortable taking such segmentation criteria public. Indeed, given that one of Green Hills' strategies was to continue pushing the boundaries of retail loyalty marketing, it was felt that the company needed to maintain as much flexibility in the "public" face of the program as possible; thus, using an airline-type loyalty structure in which the segmentation criteria is made public was not favored.

At the same time, it was felt that more structure was needed in marketing segmentations than was provided by percentage-based segments (such as the top 10% of customers based on spending). By using a defined criteria (as opposed to a percentage) to re-sort the customer base on a regular basis, Green Hills is able to benchmark their performance, able to provide year-on-year comparisons between their marketing segments.

After much trial and error, it was decided that spending and the length of time customers had shopped with the company in the past were both equally important measures in defining customer loyalty and thus in customer segments for marketing purposes. Green Hills' marketing-based customer tier segmentations then looked something like this:

(Marketing)Tier 1: A customer household that has spent $100 in the past week, OR $400 in the past 4 weeks, OR $500 in the past 10 weeks, OR $1,300 in the past 26 weeks. By building segments in this way, Green Hills is recognizing both spending and time in determining customer loyalty. Other segments (Marketing Tiers 2, 3, and so on) were built in similar fashion. Green Hills re-sorts their customer base each month.

The rationale for this segmentation is found in Green Hills' wishing to recognize new, high spending customers (as evidenced by the $100 in the past week OR $400 in the past 4 weeks), and yet also recognize customers shopping for longer periods of time, spending somewhat less per visit. By taking the calculation back 26 weeks, Green Hills found that this provided for customers going on vacation for up to several weeks, etc., the customer not penalized for being away by being dropped to a lower tier.

This structure was used internally for marketing purposes. For example, Green Hills would extend special pricing on hams at Easter time to top customer segments using this marketing-based sorting method. This segmentation criterion was never expressed publicly, as it was thought to be too confusing to try and clearly explain to consumers. Even so, this segmentation scheme offers a very powerful tool for internal marketing use.

Other Segmentation Thoughts...

Marketers can derive yet more value from any of the segmentation methods used by going one step further: subdividing each segment into those customers receiving a relatively large amount of discounts, or markdown, and those customers receiving a lesser amount. A further reason for tracking markdown expenditures is that it is very indicative of shopping behavior motivation. Those customers with a relatively high amount of markdown measured as a percentage of their total spending are likely deal-driven consumers; conversely, those customers with a lower ration of markdown to purchasing are motivated by other factors to shop with the retailer. Naturally, it is much more profitable for the retailer to engender more shopping and retention from the non-deal-driven customers within the customer base.

It is very important that customer segmentation for marketing purposes be done dynamically; it cannot be a stagnant process.

Carulla Vivero is the second largest supermarket company in Colombia, headquartered in Bogota. The company is well along in their efforts to build customer knowledge. Having a loyalty platform in two of their three formats, the company aggressively captures high levels of customer information.

During the course of my discussions with the Vivero marketing staff it became evident that they also had wrestled with how to define customer loyalty. Understanding that in many of the markets in which they operated there were many poorer neighborhoods; Vivero was uncomfortable basing loyalty segmentations on spending alone. By getting access to demographic data by customer tract (similar to a postal code segmentation), the Vivero people were able to benchmark the potential spending of consumers based on their per capita income and spending as reported in census information.

Using such information, the Vivero people ingeniously built a complex segmentation algorithm to run against their large database. They were thus able to create a Gold segment of customers, then creating a package of rewards that these customers would be entitled to. Gold customers would receive a statement each month reporting their point balances and containing targeted offers generated by the marketing database in addition to receiving other benefits over time. All told, as Vivero found out over time, these benefits, especially the direct mailings, were quite expensive to provide.

While pursuing the proper goals, a mistake was made in execution. The Vivero marketing people were correctly following the precepts of successful retail loyalty marketing: identify, recognize, and reward your most valuable customers. The mistake they made was in permanently fixing these customers as Gold in their database; once a gold customer, always a gold customer – regardless if a customer decreased or even stopped shopping with Vivero altogether. The marketing staff overlooked the fact that consumer shopping behavior is dynamic; therefore, a retailer's segmentation process needs to be equally dynamic.

This example reminds me of a retailer a number of years ago, in the early days of retail frequent shopper programs. This retailer had implemented their program to good success. Taking a cue from the airline programs, this retailer worked to establish a "Gold" card for its better customers. They publicly announced that from that day forth any customer spending over $500 would receive a "Gold" card. Just one problem: they forgot to specify a time period. What happened next was inevitable. Some higher spending customers quickly received their "Gold" card and began enjoying the associated benefits and rewards offered Gold customers. But eventually, even lower spending (lower value) customers also attained the gold threshold and qualified for both the new card and the rewards. An expensive lesson learned.

Customer-Focused Marketing Toolkit

Retailers pursuing these activities have developed extensive libraries of benefits and tools which can be extended to customers. These benefits can be categorized and sub-categorized, this framework providing a foundation for the ensuing discussion. The primary groupings that customer differentiation tactics can be divided into are two: the first involving economic differentiators, or hard benefits; the second, termed soft benefits, encompassing the areas of services, privileges and recognition. Each of the two primary categories can be further divided into those benefits that are earned by the consumer, typically by meeting specified shopping criteria (spend $X within a certain period of time), and those benefits awarded for past shopping.

In larger companies it is helpful to add the following constructs to the assembling of such initiatives. Experience has shown that hard benefits are best coordinated at the company headquarters or regional office level; this is done to control the financial cost incurred by such marketing efforts. Soft benefits are often much more powerful when executed at the local level, store level, or even a department or category level. Relationships are between people, such as the relationship between a sales clerk and a regular customer. Efforts at recognizing high value customers are much more powerful, and genuine, when carried out at the local level where the customer may expect to be recognized for being a regular shopper. Economic benefits typically help serve to augment relationships with high value customers; almost by definition such customers are not deal-driven, preferring a retailer for other attributes.

Customer-focused initiatives can be effective at each level of a company; from the headquarters to division or regional offices, and further to individual stores and even departments within a store. Certainly, as mentioned earlier, specific programs are best coordinated and executed at varying levels within the organization.

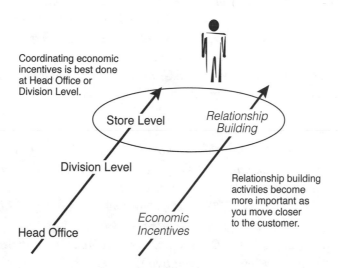

Coordinating economic incentives is best done at Head Office or Division Level.

Store Level

Relationship Building

Division Level

Relationship building activities become more important as you move closer to the customer.

Head Office

Economic Incentives

Eventually a retailer begins to discover that their most valuable customers may not be motivated by discounts or other monetary rewards. By thinking outside the box in the area of privileges and services, retailers can now recognize their highest value customers with other meaningful offerings.

Each February, come Valentine's Day, M&M Meat Shops store owners personally deliver a bouquet of roses to each of their top customers. While some franchisees were uncomfortable the first year this was done, the enthusiastic responses of their customers soon overrode such thoughts. The word of mouth generated by this simple activity was incalculable.

Copper Mountain, a Colorado ski resort, offers the Beeline Advantage service to guests of the resort's lodges, or those willing to pay premium prices for lift tickets. Beeline Advantage holders have their own dedicated lift line, allowing them to bypass the crowd. These best customers can get on the lifts 15 minutes before they open to the public each morning, in addition to having VIP lines in the ski equipment rental shops.

Rather than go to market selling Easter hams at below-cost retail prices, Green Hills now mails its Tier 1 customers a postcard informing them they may purchase a premium quality ham at a very attractive price; this benefit is only for best customers, not the public at large.

Rice Epicurean Markets store managers deliver fresh food baskets to their very best customers at home just prior to the holidays. This is in addition to mailing personally-signed holiday cards to their best customers.

During a recent holiday season, BCBG, an upscale women's clothing store, sent certain customers a rich offer for a $100 savings on any purchase of $200 or more.

DSW Shoe Warehouse rewards their customers with a $25 Gift Certificate each time the customer accumulates $250 in purchases. Because shoe buying is not a frequent activity, DSW does not specify a time period during which the purchases must be made. They do, however, specify that the reward certificate, once earned, be used within several months of issue. While the certificate had to be used relatively soon, the purchase made with it counted toward the next-earned reward offered by DSW.

Shoppers Drug Mart of Canada periodically runs sweepstakes contests designed to recognize and reward their best customers. For example, during one program customers received an entry into a sweepstakes each time they used their Shoppers Optimum Card and spent more than CND$20 (pretax) when buying specified items. The more often the customer shops, the more entries they would receive in the contest.

Many retail companies take good advantage of their ability to now reward customers for their shopping over time. These programs are typically referred to as either reward programs or threshold programs, as customers must meet some level of spending criteria within a specified period of time to qualify. Rewards used in threshold programs can take many forms. These types of programs, used by a multitude of retail companies in several sectors, offer incentive for customers to centralize their purchasing within a given sector with the retailer during the time of the program. While a few customers may only ramp up their purchasing to earn the rewards and then revert to their old pattern, many customers maintain a more frequent, and higher purchasing, level.

Pegi Klein-Weber of M&M Meat Shops has had great success in working with various consumer goods manufacturers in support of her company's customer-focused marketing efforts. In the first MAX reward program, M&M offered a

CDN$10 and $20 gift certificate as the reward for customers achieving pecified spending thresholds. The next program used an electric knife made by Hamilton Beach with a stated retail value of CDN$17.00; M&M Meat Shops was able to obtain a substantial quantity for much less. This threshold program required customers to spend $250 during a 10 week period; the winners were then notified by mail to pick up their knife at their local M&M shop.

This example brings to light an important question: what types of rewards work best for these types of programs? While there is no simple answer appropriate for all retail channels, there are some guidelines when executing these types of threshold reward programs.

First, the perceived value of the reward is what will motivate customers to modify their shopping behavior so as to earn the reward. For several years now, Green Hills has awarded a free premium quality Christmas tree to its customers who have spent over $1,000 during the annual Thanksgiving Turkey program. While the tree has a perceived value of $50, the cost to Green Hills is much less.

Secondly, rewards that have as universal an appeal as possible will result in greater success than those that do not. For example, at M&M Meat Shops, thought was given to using a free M&M Meat Shops product as the reward, such as a frozen apple pie. While some people might enjoy apple pie, others may prefer blueberry; apple pie may not have a broad appeal.

Third, it is strongly recommended that retailers do not run the same threshold reward program consecutively. M&M Meat Shops' first program offered a gift certificate as the reward incentive; the second program, an electric knife. The third program used an insulated cooler, timed for the summer barbecuing season. Retailers that have run the same, or very similar, program over and over have found that subsequent programs result in diminishing success and return on investment. The first time a program is offered it is something novel and unique to customers; the second time it is well-worn.

Successful practitioners do not overuse this tactic. These companies may run between one and three reward programs over the course of the year, perhaps seasonally or in synchrony with business patterns.

When executing such customer-focused marketing tactics, experience has provided several beneficial lessons. Most successful practitioners have learned that it is best to go to market using a mix of benefits, dividing them between those benefits that are earned by the customer (typically by spending specified monies), and those that are provided as "surprise" benefits (awarded in appreciation for past performance).

Successful retailers work to create a "library" of rewards or incentives that they can look to use over time. A best practice in this regard is the development of a marketing calendar designed to lay out over the year what benefits will be provided when to the company's customers. Going further, retailers using this will break out the different benefits provided (hard versus soft) and also distinguish as earned benefits or appreciation for past behaviors.

Customer Focused Marketing as a Process

One of the most important assets gained through the capture of customer data lies in the ability to measure customer shopping over time. This has particular impact on the area of marketing as companies can now begin to relate changes in shopping behavior directly to their marketing and operational processes. Because they now have feedback in the form of measurable customer shopping, retail companies can begin to apply the principles of process improvement to their marketing activities.

Shortly before his death in 1993 I attended one of W. Edwards Deming's famous four day seminars in Total Quality Management. Deming is considered by many to be the father of Total Quality Management and its continuous process improvement philosophy. Taking a page from Deming's work, retailers can apply the concept to their customer-focused marketing efforts.

To see how this process can be utilized, we shall look at the new customer segment. By first putting in place a system to measure the inflow of new customers and the retention of the new customers over time (for example, the first year), a company is able to create baseline information to measure against future results. Once the measurement system is in place, companies can then proceed to design marketing and operational processes seeking to improve the retention of the new customers over time (impacting the inflow of new customers is a separate process). Following the tenants of process improvement, the company should then monitor the impact of their efforts, regularly altering the program to improve results. [1]

Process Improvement Applied to Customer-Focused Marketing and Retention of New Customers

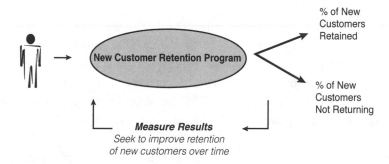

While the example here relates to new customers, the concept can be applied to many areas. For example, a company may wish to focus marketing on customers declining in their spending, designing incentives and communications targeted to those customers. By measuring their results, for example the percentage of targeted customers who increase their spending or are retained by the company, the marketer can work to improve their process, seeking to foster even stronger results.

Additional Evaluation Methods

There are additional ways to measure the veracity of marketing programs or promotions beyond the customer inventory and tier analysis tools. Many retail companies make use of the following methods.

Measuring Effectiveness Through Control Groups...

In the retail world, marketing analysts have made use of control groups for evaluating the effectiveness of certain marketing programs. Control groups involve the creation of two identical, or nearly identical, customer segments; one group receiving an offer or incentive, the other customer group not receiving the offer. By monitoring the resulting changes in behavior, and comparing the group receiving the offer against the control group, analysts may show the effectiveness of making the offer.

This method is a proven tool for use in the evaluation of database marketing-driven programs and is widely accepted by analysts and marketing people. We have seen this tool widely used by large retail companies who have created regular mailing programs containing targeted offers to various customer segments. The control group methodology is used to calculate the return on investment of such offers.

Gains, as measured using a control group methodology, are often expressed as incremental, the offer generating some increase in spending when evaluated against the control group. Though gains may indeed be realized, what occurs in practice is that further programs are undertaken based upon the incremental returns; companies decide that as long as the incremental gain is greater than the incremental cost to generate it, the program is effective.

The difficulty I have seen arise from this practice is that in many cases these marketing programs continue to be incremental; they are added on to all the other marketing activities the companies have made use of. While there may indeed be a gain, these companies are failing to capture the far-greater gains to be had from a more comprehensive customer approach; marketing efforts directly aimed at increasing the number of customer households shopping, increasing customers' spending, and increasing retention of valuable customers.

Before-During-After Analyses...

Another popular method used for evaluating the effectiveness of marketing programs is referred to as a Before-During-After analysis. Such an analysis is self-evident; the company looks at the same customers' behavior during a marketing program and compares the customers' shopping behavior to the time period before and after the promotion. Obviously, one must be aware of holidays or other events that may skew customer behavior.

For example, one retail company ran a reward program offering customers spending above a certain threshold ($250) a premium. Applying the Before-During-After analysis method produced the following report.

Program Qualifiers	10 weeks prior to threshold	10 weeks of program	10 weeks after program
# of Customer Households	9,792 83%	11,868 100%	10,954 92%
Total Spending	$1,883,197.00	$3,913,473.00	$2,080,603.00
Avg. $ / HH % increase	$192.32	$329.75 71%	$189.94
# transactions avg. trans per HH % increase	43,575 4.45	74,765 6.3 42%	47,613 4.35
Avg. $/Trans.	$43.22	$52.35 21%	$43.70

The report shows us that 11,868 customers took part in the promotion, spending the required threshold amount of $250 (or more). In total, these customers generated $3,913,473.00 in sales, producing an average spending per customer household of $329.75 during the promotion.

Of the 11,868 customers participating, 9,792 of them shopped in the period before the promotion. As we can see, the average spending per customer household increased 71% during the promotion. Additionally, the number of transactions (shopping frequency) increased 42% during the promotion. We can also see the customers' behavior in the period after the promotion.

A simple return on investment calculation for the program can be made by applying the additional gross profit realized from the increase in sales to the cost of the promotion. In this example, applying the company's gross profit margin to the additional nearly $2 million in sales volume generated during the program, and then subtracting the related costs, provides the company their return on investment.

This type analysis begins to bring to light other questions. Notice that only 83% of the participants shopped in the before period compared to 92% of them in the after period. Where did these additional customers come from? Did the promotion attract new customers? Do these types of programs increase customer retention in the time after the promotion?

The Lifetime Value Conundrum...

In the mail order industry, the use of customer lifetime value is an established practice to assist in the return on investment calculation relative to marketing initiatives. If a database marketer knows the typical spending of a group of customers, and is able to forecast how well the company is able to retain said customers over time (usually years), it is possible to project the future income stream from the customer group and bring it back to a present value. Using this calculation, marketers measure the effectiveness of new campaigns to attract new customers or to influence spending or frequency of ordering.

A number of people have tried to apply the same rationale and calculations to retail database work. Retail companies possessing some history of customer data certainly know their customers' spending and are able to project customer retention. The challenge of attempting to apply this concept to the retail world lies in the assumptions made.

In the direct mail industry, customer behavior is relatively stable over time; companies are able to develop reasonably accurate projections in regard to customer behavior with some degree of confidence they will bear out over time. This is particularly true when projecting customer behavior out over several years, typically needed in lifetime value calculations.

Retail is much more dynamic. A retail company investing a sum of money in a marketing campaign, and using lifetime value to justify the expenditure, is much more at risk of customer behavior changing when looking out over a several year period. If a new competitor opens up nearby that was not forecast, it will have a substantial impact upon customer shopping behavior; chances are customer retention will be adversely affected. Likewise, if a price war breaks out in a given market, customer behavior will be heavily impacted.

The lifetime value equation is often used when developing campaigns to acquire new customers. In the mail order industry, companies realize that if they are able to generate a 5% redemption rate in a new customer acquisition campaign, the lifetime value of those acquired can be used to evaluate the return on investment of the effort. The mail order company knows that the new customers are the result of a specific mailing; there is no bad data. Transferring this practice to mass retail is much harder; are new customers coming into stores the result of the latest ad flyer, radio campaign, television advertising, or their next door neighbor prompting them? It is nearly impossible to isolate the reason prompting a new customer visit, thus making it very difficult to use lifetime value to calculate a return on investment.

Perhaps in place of lifetime value calculations, marketing departments can utilize the customer inventory reporting tool presented earlier.

Along this line, we would propose an alternative to the forward-looking lifetime value measurement by creating a backwards-looking opportunity cost measurement. A company would start by segmenting lapsed customers into tiers; how many of the lapsed customers in a given period were formerly from Tier 1, Tier 2, and so on. Once knowing this, it is relatively easy to assign a monetary value to these lost customers; the retailer knows the annualized spending of Tier 1 customers, etc. The company then knows the opportunity cost associated with losing these customers and can work to develop initiatives to either bring them back or to prevent them from leaving in the first place, having a good measure to use in calculating return on investment.

Customer-Focused Marketing: Additional Considerations

Public or Stealth:

While there are endless ways for a retailer to define customer groups or to segment customers for marketing purposes, companies must give further thought to how they wish to execute their initiatives: will such efforts be publicly announced, or will they be of a more stealthy nature? Will the retailer now state publicly that they will recognize and reward their regular customers through their loyalty platform, or will they communicate directly to the customer, e.g. mailing the customer a letter informing them that they are valued and enclosing some type of special offer or recognition?

Best practices have evolved that indicate the use of earned benefits should be done in a public fashion: any consumer may qualify simply by meeting the specified spending and time criteria. Soft benefits and financial-based offers of appreciation are best carried out through stealth modes: delivering notice to the customer by way of direct mail, e-mail, via kiosks in a store or some other direct-to-individual consumer method. It is still wise to keep in mind when developing such initiatives that the occasion may arise when a store associate will have to offer an explanation to a consumer asking why their neighbor received a certain offer and they did not; having a ready and prepared response is good planning.

Some retail companies may wish to tie together their internal threshold segmentations with their external marketing efforts. For example, a company could publicly state that any customer household spending more than $1,000.00 during the quarter (using specific dates) would become a "Preferred" customer, thus qualifying for specified benefits and rewards. Running such a program, the retailer is able to make their customer tier definitions the same for both financial reporting and marketing purposes. By going to market this way, a retailer is offering the consumer the ability to self-select their participation in the retailer's program.

While such a marketing strategy facilitates the understanding of customer tier definitions by a retailer's staff, helping them align internal reporting with inquisitive customers, there can also be challenges in utilizing this tactic. By publicly stating their performance / reward structure, retailers are telegraphing their tactics to competitors. As an example, let's return to the airline frequent flyer programs. If airline A requires a passenger to fly 50,000 miles in a calendar year to become a "Gold" frequent flyer and receive specified benefits, the airline has informed competing airlines of their marketing tactics. One can easily imagine airline B decreasing the qualifying mileage to 40,000 miles or increasing the rewards. It is just this situation that is behind the "stealth" e-mail communications between airlines and their frequent flyers; the airlines offer their best customers deals that are not for everyone.

There is no right or wrong strategy here for retailers. The choice between public or stealth customer segmentation is an almost philosophical discussion; the correct choice being the one that best fits the company's culture, both internally and with their customers.

Build a Historical Record

My experience working in this area for most of the past decade has taught me that a great deal of the value relative to collecting and using customer data in retail lies in building a historical record of marketing, advertising, and promotional activities alongside a record of customer activity. It is amazing how some things become obvious when reviewing activities over time, things which may not have been readily apparent at the time they were taking place.

Creating a record of advertising activities (newspaper, radio, television, etc.) and a record of customer focused marketing efforts (best customer recognition, reward programs, etc.) and linking them together with customer household counts, customer retention measures, customer spending within each tier, and so on, can provide an invaluable resource for companies over time.

Closely related is the idea of building a history of case studies, each case study a customer focused marketing activity that was carried out. On many occasions I have seen companies execute a number of marketing programs designed to impact on customer shopping, but the companies then failed to take the time to analyze and evaluate each effort. Experience is the best teacher of all.

REQUIREMENTS FOR SUCCESS

The world of retail presents a very different environment in which to proactively gather, understand, and use customer data from other business formats. Customer relationship management (CRM) has become a much-pursued process in many channels, from such financial services as banking and insurance to the tourism industry (airlines, hotels, car rental, etc.), in both business-to-business models and business-to-consumer models.

Many of these other businesses have a head start, already possessing a great deal of information about their individual customers. For these companies, the challenge lies in assembling their disparate data into a useable form, allowing them to identify areas of opportunity. For example, insurance companies know their customers' names and addresses, in addition to the value of their homes, automobiles, and other personal possessions. Many times they also gather income data and other confidential information as part of the selling process.

CRM efforts in such businesses tend to be more low-key: an occasional letter describing other services offered; a phone call offering to upgrade the customer to a Gold credit card; or an e-mail informing the customer of the latest software release.

Compare this with a typical mass retail store, a much more dynamic environment

Retailing is an incredibly competitive business. Whether it is clothing with its added pressures of fashion trends, convenience stores at risk of channel erosion, drug stores facing similar issues, or food retailing, which has nearly become a true commodity business in which lowest price wins, retail requires doing many things right simply to be in the game. Regardless of the channel, retail stores must offer a clean environment, well-stocked shelves, products of some level of quality, and a modicum of customer service. Failing in any of these will endanger a retail business very quickly.

In addition, add to the mix personnel pressures: service staff positions paying minimum wage or slightly above; an undereducated workforce not cognizant of the latest in interpersonal communication skills. For many retailers, simply finding a body that's breathing to fill positions is difficult.

Now into this pressure-cooker environment let's throw customer relationship management: identifying customers each time they shop, and relying upon the service staff to properly recognize and reward valued shoppers. It is no wonder that, in a recent study done in the supermarket channel, nearly 70% of CEO's reported dissatisfaction with their customer loyalty programs.[1] Nevertheless, nearly all stated that their loyalty marketing efforts remain a very important initiative. While the goals are worthy, the challenges are immense.

Yet it is this same intense and dynamic environment that offers great opportunity to those companies able to rise to the challenge. Consumers purchase insurance annually and typically choose banking relationships even less frequently. But these same consumers grocery shop several times per week, visit drug stores regularly, make clothing purchases at least seasonally, and must fuel their cars often. It is this dynamic shopping behavior that offers retailers great opportunity in the form of influencing these behaviors to the store's benefit.

SUCCESS FACTORS

In my observations working with companies in several channels across various markets throughout the world, it is readily apparent that to be successful in retailing requires not only a sound strategy, but also a discipline in operations and execution of strategy. The hypercompetitive world of retail today no longer forgives companies who are slack in their operations or unfocused in their chosen realm.

Retailers wishing to embark on a journey of gathering, understanding, and using customer information in how they do business must, to succeed, view it as a business strategy; a strategy involving their entire organization, and one requiring a long term perspective.

While there are a tremendous number of details related to the collection and use of customer data that can determine the degree of success, there are four primary requirements for success that must be heeded for a company to employ customer intelligence. They are:

1) Top management understanding and commitment.
2) The redirection of some portion of mass marketing expenditures to fund customer focused activities.
3) Gathering enough accurate customer data.
4) Remembering that it is all about the customer.

1) Understanding and Commitment...

Inevitably, one of the most important factors in the success or failure of such an initiative is the understanding and commitment of the owners or top management team of the business. This applies whether it is a single store operation or one of the largest retailers in the world. For a retailer of any size to successfully practice customer intelligent retailing, the entire organization must be committed to the gathering, understanding, and use of customer data. The discipline required to do this properly must be driven from the top, each level of management held responsible for their roles in the process.

To provide an example, the top management team of one of the larger supermarket retailers in the U.S. now looks at customer metrics every week as part of their management reporting. This company has committed to this business strategy, and is now measuring and managing their business by customer metrics in addition to their management measures of old.

Contrast this practice with a division of another large food retailer, whose price-based loyalty platform requires the use of the company's frequent shopper card to receive the special advertised prices. The head of this division, not appreciating the value of customer data, actually advocates the use of a miscellaneous frequent shopper card at the front end, enabling customers not carrying or wanting to have the retailer's card to receive the special prices. In many ways, this company executive is undermining the very essence of customer intelligence within his company.

The requirements for gathering, understanding, and using customer data effectively manifest themselves throughout a retail organization. From the need for marketing departments to redirect some mass marketing expenditures to fund customer-focused initiatives, to the need for discipline in having to use one's card to obtain special prices or to collect points, top management must be steadfast in their commitment to customer knowledge.

Companies are striving to propagate customer knowledge through each level of their companies; from head office, to regional or division levels, and, ultimately, to the individual store. To accomplish this successfully requires top management to actively drive customer knowledge through their organizations.

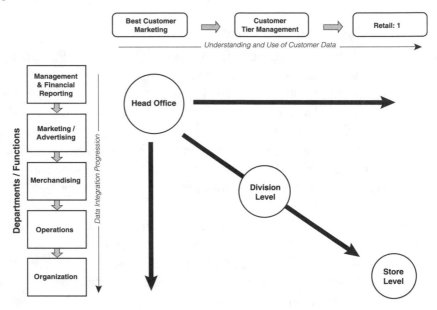

It is this challenge of making the use of customer-based measures and information central to operations through each level of an organization that is perhaps the largest hurdle, as well as the greatest opportunity. Distributing reports is easy; employee comprehension is not. Educating personnel throughout the company in each level of the organization as to understanding the data is management's most important task. Further, coaching and discussion relative to what to do with the data once understood is paramount; what good are new tools if people do not know how to make use of them?

During M&M Meat Shops' annual convention, workshops were arranged for the store owners and managers; rather than one large meeting, the attendees were divided into smaller groups, allowing for more discussion. The sessions were devoted to a thorough review of each customer-based management report provided the stores; from an explanation of each number reported and how it is calculated to a wide-ranging discussion on how to use the reports and what to look for. Each workshop also included thoughts and discussion related to using this information in how the stores went to market. Similar information is being uploaded to the company's internal website, making it accessible to all franchisees and managers.

Other leading companies engender a similar commitment to fostering the education and understanding of customer-based information throughout their organizations. Rice Epicurean Markets held several meetings with company and store level management to completely explain and discuss these new measures; each person left the meeting armed with notes and written materials to refer to later. Select Japanese retailers are engaging in a similar process with people from throughout their companies.

Sam Azout, President of Carulla-Vivero (Bogota, Colombia), brought together the management, marketing, and procurement staffs from each of his organizations for a day-long conference and discussion, further reinforced with follow up materials. These leaders have backed up their stated commitment to a business strategy based upon customer intelligence with action.

Top management must also be committed to putting in place the necessary technologies to capture and use customer information.

Technology

Technology has become a strategic weapon for some retailers. Wal-Mart has used technology to develop world-class solutions to tracking and measuring their product supply chain from point of manufacture to the store's shelf. And they control this cost at every point, providing them the lowest cost structures amongst retailers in their channel.

Technology as a fulcrum of strategy can be a double-edged sword, as many companies in the convenience store sector are finding. Convenience store operators are in many cases held hostage by the oil companies' control of their point of sale systems and pumping technology. Many of these systems were developed decades ago by the oil companies so as to track the sale of gas at the pump, and then integrate this to a POS system in the store and into payment channels; using your credit card at the pump is many times a technology that has its core in software code and hardwired systems developed decades ago.

Because many of the POS systems are proprietary, owned and controlled by the large oil companies, convenience store operators have little ability to modify the system so as to support a customer intelligence initiative. It is extremely difficult for the operators to capture a customer identifier or to gather sku level data and move it to a database. Their hands are tied.

These convenience store operators were appalled to learn that supermarkets, now entering the gasoline trade, are not tied to these legacy systems. The supermarkets have forced development of technologies, allowing them to view the gas being sold in the parking lot as just another product and the pump as an alternative POS terminal. They are able to completely integrate their gasoline and grocery store marketing efforts. Customers can prepay for gas in the store, the value then being loaded on their loyalty card for use at the pump outside. Retailers reward their customers for their fuel purchasing over time with food rewards, and vice versa.

The convenience store operators left the meeting that day with a great appreciation for how technology can become a strategic weapon, or a competitive Achilles' heel.

Retail companies pursuing the gathering, understanding, and use of customer data must be willing to put in place the systems necessary to not only capture such information across their operations, but also to cost-effectively communicate with their customers.

The Peril of Pilot Programs

When evaluating the strategy of developing customer intelligence, many larger retail companies give thought to creating a pilot or test program within a store grouping or division. At times these efforts are successful, providing the retail company an opportunity to test tactics and technologies; other times such efforts are doomed from their conception.

ASDA, during the mid to late 1990s, was the only large supermarket retailer in the U.K. market not to have a loyalty platform. Management created a pilot program, launching the ASDA Clubcard program in about twenty stores. While the loyalty team within ASDA executed a number of marketing initiatives based upon the use of customer data gathered through the program, the results were not convincing enough to move forward.

Part of the reason behind this failure was the original design and structure of the program itself. The ASDA Clubcard essentially mimicked the other loyalty programs operating in the U.K. market at the time; all points-based programs that essentially provided a 1% rebate to the consumer. Before any change in consumer shopping behavior, such programs must generate a substantial increase in turnover or profit margins simply to offset the cost of the base program.

ASDA held a strong position in the market as a low price leader; the adoption of a points-based loyalty scheme did nothing to reinforce this market position; if anything, it fought against it. Furthermore, as was discussed earlier, retail companies must redirect some portion of their marketing expenditures to capitalize on the opportunity provided by customer knowledge. In the pilot program of ASDA, such a redirection was nearly impossible as the rest of the company continued to go to market as it always had, low prices for everyone.

Time and again we see that successful practitioners of customer intelligence commit their entire organizations to this strategy. Senior management must resist the impulse to create pilot programs or study the concept to death.

2) Customer-Focused Marketing Economics... the need to redirect spending!

The past decade has been witness to an explosion of Best Customer marketing efforts in retail, particularly in the supermarket channel where loyalty marketing has been in place for some years. While many such programs have been successful, there are lessons provided by both successful and unsuccessful initiatives.

Rewarding best customer behavior has become commonplace in some retail channels, a favored tactic being some type of reward program enabled through the loyalty platform. These efforts typically require the customer to meet certain behavior criteria, such as spending a specified amount of money or accumulating a certain number of points within a fixed time period, in order to qualify for some reward. In addition to these type programs, retailers have employed a mix of other economic-based and service-based benefits to recognize their favored customers.

Rice Epicurean Markets has carried out a number of customer-focused marketing efforts aimed at encouraging customers to centralize their shopping with the retailer. One of these efforts, rewarding customers with a 5% discount certificate for every $300 in spending during a certain time period, has evolved into a favorite – both for the company and for customers.

But Rice Epicurean has not just layered the expense of this customer-focused program onto their past marketing expenditures. Rather, the company has been able to reduce monies spent on mass marketing vehicles, such as ad flyers and newspaper advertising, and instead redirected these savings into funding their new initiatives.

This change is graphically represented in Figure 6-1. Inverting the pyramid on the right, redirecting marketing expenditures to the more valuable customers, is now referred to as Customer-Focused Marketing Economics.

Figure 6-1   **Customer-Focused Marketing Economics:**

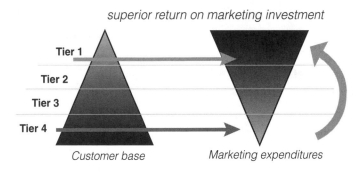

Companies practicing best customer marketing have many times been doing the correct thing in focusing on their more valuable customers, rewarding and recognizing them, thus realizing more purchases and greater profit margins. The downside has been that these same companies have often layered this expense on top of their other marketing expenditures; they have failed to redirect their marketing monies. These companies have in a very real sense offset the profit gains provided by such a strategy through increasing their overall marketing expenditures.

One Kroger division located in California, Ralphs, made use of Web Miles, an internet-based company which sold air miles, redeemable on any airline, to retailers for use as incentives in loyalty efforts. Ralphs was a large customer of Web Miles prior to Web Miles' going out of business, in part because of Ralphs' exit from the program.

The basic program was straightforward; consumers would register their Ralphs Club card number with Web Miles, participants then earning one mile for each dollar spent during the program. In addition, consumers could also earn miles shopping at other retail merchants as well as online retailers. Consumers could check their miles balance through their online account and redeem miles through the Web Miles site. Ralphs in turn paid Web Miles each month for the miles awarded to its customers.

Ralphs executed a promotion through the Web Miles program which rewarded certain customers double miles for achieving a specified spending amount in a certain time period; the reward necessitated a substantial increase in spending behavior. The results of the initiative were quite impressive, creating a very significant gain in customer spending and producing a solid return on investment for the program. One of the benefits to the Web Miles format was that it enabled the use of e-mail communication with customers, thereby eliminating costly direct mail.

So where did Ralphs (Kroger) go wrong? Ralphs was directed to substantially reduce marketing expenditures by the Kroger head office, as it was working to cut $500 million annually from its cost structure to further its price competitiveness with Wal-Mart. Given such a directive, Ralphs had little choice but to cut the Web Miles program, as Kroger considered this a marketing expenditure. Rather than looking to reduce markdown expense, much of which fosters deal-dependent customers, and redirecting those monies to fund program such as Web Miles which can help create higher spending, more profitable customers, Ralphs / Kroger killed off a powerful tool.

Retailers that practice best customer marketing, but simply add these initiatives on top of all their other traditional marketing efforts, are falling prey to what we can refer to as "Add-on" Marketing Economics, as represented in Figure 6-2.

Figure 6-2 **Customer-Focused Marketing Economics:**

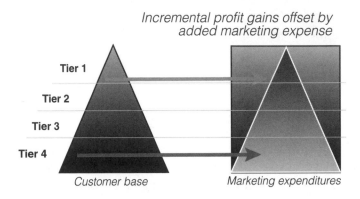

Incremental profit gains offset by added marketing expense

Tier 1
Tier 2
Tier 3
Tier 4

Customer base   *Marketing expenditures*

Such a shift in marketing expenditures represents a profound change; it is the rare marketing department that willingly moves away from traditional methods. While there are marketing people that believe in the power of customer-based marketing, and proactively drive these changes in going to market, more times than not such directives must emanate from top management.

To maximize return on investment, retail companies must redirect some portion of their past mass marketing expenditures to funding their customer-focused marketing activities.

Traditional Marketing Budget	*Marketing Budget Re-Directing $ to Include Customer-Focused Activities*		*"Add-On" Customer-Focused Marketing Activities*	
Ad Flyer production & distribution: $500,000.00	Ad Flyer production & distribution:	$400,000.00	Ad Flyer production & distribution:	$500,000.00
Radio $300,000.00	Radio	$200,000.00	Radio	$300,000.00
Television $150,000.00	Television	$75,000.00	Television	$150,000.00
Billboards $50,000.00	Billboards	$25,000.00	Billboards	$50,000.00
	Customer-Focused Marketing Activities	*$300,000.00*	*Customer-Focused Marketing Activities*	*$300,000.00*
Total Marketing Budget: $1,000,000.00	Total Marketing Budget: $1,000,000.00		Total Marketing Budget: $1,300,000.00	
	This company will maximize the gain in gross profit margins to their bottom lines because they have not increased their overall marketing expenditures.		*This company has negated some portion of their gross margin gains through layering on their customer-focused marketing activities, thus increasing their costs.*	

It has been frustration with the perceived lack of payback relative to their loyalty efforts that has led some retailers to drop their programs. In many cases this has been the correct decision; unless a retailer is willing to alter their marketing economics and redirect, they are simply increasing their cost structure by operating a loyalty platform. Needless to say, companies that have not developed this basic discipline typically do not further advance their understanding and use of customer data in their operations.

Robin Clark, editor of The Wise Marketer (thewisemarketer.com), ran a telling story of Delvita, a supermarket chain in the Czech Republic. Delvita launched a loyalty program in 1996 in response to the entry of Tesco and Carrefour into its markets. While the company issued over 1 million cards and was identifying approximately 80% of turnover through its loyalty program, Delvita made the decision in 2001 to discontinue its program due to the high cost and lack of return on investment. [2]

Through customer surveys, Delvita found that many of its customers said they would shop with the company regardless of the program and many found that the program offered too little in its rewards. While the company used such information as further justification for terminating the Karta Delvita Plus program, other reasons may be the root cause.

The first problem may have been the structure of the program itself: a points program resulting in a 1% rebate to customers – hardly original when competing against Tesco, who has used such a program for years. Further, and perhaps most importantly, Delvita admitted that it was difficult and expensive to process the data in a meaningful fashion, and the company had problems measuring increased profitability from changes in customer behavior.

The situation at Delvita is one commonly found amongst retail companies attempting to work with customer information. Management instinctively realizes that such data should be valuable, but, lacking the proper reporting structure, simply drowns in the data, not knowing how to measure what is happening and if their efforts are paying dividends or not.

This same frustration with return on investment has led even more companies to banish the loyalty program to the marketing department, where it many times originated in the first place. Top management sees some benefit to retaining their retail loyalty platform, but it has lost its place as the golden child in the organization. Its usefulness is now limited to helping control markdown expense (in price-based programs) and providing some occasional customer data beyond that offered by surveys and focus groups.

3) Gather Enough (Accurate!) Information

The next primary ingredient necessary for success is gathering enough customer data. On many occasions I have observed and met with companies expressing interest in pursuing a customer-focused strategy, and yet they do not have the systems and processes in place to provide for the necessary information, or they have corrupted their information-gathering systems with false data. Like the large regional retail company who stated that they were identifying 85% of total sales back to individual customers – until it was discovered that they made use of miscellaneous loyalty cards at their checkouts for customers not having or wanting a card. We found these miscellaneous cards were accounting for over 15-20% of total sales, giving the company a true capture rate of only 65-70%.

Retail companies have an increasing array of customer touch-points through which they are able to gather such detailed customer information. From proprietary credit cards to check cashing, from online transactions to biometric payment methods, from call centers to loyalty programs, retailers have an incredible flow of customer data, should they wish to tap it.

Consider what is happening around the world relative to customer information...

Home Depot has over 11 million consumer and commercial credit accounts using its private credit card. Those cards accounted for approximately 22% of Home Depot's 2002 sales; i.e. Home Depot, if it is not already, can identify the individual consumers and the items and services they are buying for 22% of its total sales. [3]

Target has recently spent millions of dollars issuing new Target co-branded Visa cards containing a smart chip, issuing over 2.5 million cards by the middle of 2002 and plans for many more. In addition, the company has installed 40,000 smart card readers at each of its checkout lanes interconnected with its POS system. Going even further, Target has supplied each of its customers receiving a new card a free chip card-reader to connect to their home computer. [4] With such a device, customers will be able to download electronic coupons and other information to be stored on their cards for their next shopping trip, during which the electronic coupon is redeemed. There is little doubt that such a comprehensive system will also supply Target vast quantities of detailed customer data.

Thriftway Markets of Seattle, Washington, allows its customers to enroll in a payment system which links their fingerprint scan to a credit card, allowing the consumer to pay for their orders at the POS by simply scanning their finger. McDonald's in Fresno, California is testing a similar scheme. Kroger has been testing a finger scan check approval system for some time now in one of its divisions. Each of these types of systems will allow the retailer to capture shopping information each time the consumer scans their finger at the POS, thus identifying themselves to the retailer. Biometric-linked payment schemes are also growing in the convenience store channel.

Starbucks has issued millions of prepaid cards which consumers can use to purchase their next coffee. Such cards are expected to allow the company to begin gathering customer shopping behavior data and also serve as a platform for incentive programs and other marketing efforts.

McDonald's of Hawaii has operated a loyalty scheme for several years now based on a rewritable card system from Visible Results of New Zealand; the same system employed by petrol stations, convenience stores, restaurants, and other retail businesses throughout New Zealand, Australia, and Asia. [5]

And let's not forget about retail frequent shopper programs. A majority of supermarket companies in the U.S. now offer such programs. Kroger, Safeway, and Ahold are all committed to retail loyalty programs throughout their companies in each of their divisions. Albertson's, until recently the last big holdout, has been operating a trial in the Dallas, Texas, market, and has begun rolling out their program across other divisions. Most of the large regional supermarket companies operate such loyalty programs, along with a host of smaller retailers. Through such programs, retailers are able to capture vast quantities of detailed customer shopping data. Detailed shopping information on well over 100 million U.S. households is residing in supermarket company databases across the country.

Ahold's Stop & Shop division has signed on with Exxon to allow its customers to register their Speedpass® for use at Stop & Shop's checkouts; the Speedpass® linked to the customer's loyalty card. McDonald's is testing the same Speedpass® system in certain stores.

These types of programs have spread to chain drug stores; CVS has an ExtraCare loyalty program in place in addition to Rite Aid's Rite Rewards program and Duane Reade's Dollar Rewards Club. Boots, the U.K.-based pharmacy chain, operates its Boots Advantage Card, making extensive use of the detailed customer information gathered through its respected program. And the list goes on and on; from bookstores to casinos, retailers are identifying customers at every turn.

It is important to realize that such activities are occurring worldwide. While frequent shopper programs have been active in the U.S. and Europe for much of the past decade, interest in such activities continues to spread around the world. Asia, in particular, Japan, has seen explosive growth in retail loyalty programs as merchants look for any lifeline available as global competitors enter their marketplace.

Clearly, technology is enabling retailers to identify consumers each time they transact business and to capture and store the detailed item level information of each transaction.

We should note that a number of retail companies, particularly in Asia, operate frequent shopper or loyalty programs that are simply promotional in nature; i.e., they do not provide for the capture of detailed customer data, and most do not even develop customer contact data. While any merit to such "quasi" loyalty programs is arguable, these types of schemes are not relevant to our discussions here as they do not provide for the on-going capture of transaction-level data identified to a consumer.

To develop customer intelligence as an effective business strategy, retailers need to collect great amounts of data, identifying large percentages of their total sales and transactions to individual customers. World-class retailers are identifying over 90% of their total sales to individual customers, obtaining detailed transaction level data from their POS systems in the stores and from online transactions. When we speak of the gathering of customer information we are specifically referring to the ability to identify the customer (or house-hold) by name, some level of contact information (address, phone number, or, increasingly, e-mail address), and marrying this customer identification to each transaction the customer is involved in.

Some leading experts seem to disregard the idea of developing and using customer-based business metrics. Yet these same experts accept the validity of POS scanning data without second thought. Why? To maintain accurate and high levels of product scan data requires operational discipline. The same type of discipline can be applied to the capturing of customer information.

While we will discuss in more detail the form such customer information gathering platforms can take, there are some tactics that simply do not provide enough customer data to allow a retailer to develop customer knowledge.

We have seen retailers, many from the discount and department store channels, attempt to develop an effective loyalty program based upon their proprietary payment cards. With few exceptions, such a strategy has proven to be ineffective in gathering enough customer data to serve a customer intelligent strategy. Typically, a retailer's proprietary payment card accounts for less than 5-10% of total sales, severely limiting the retailer's view of customers' shopping habits. Given this, the Lillian Vernon Company's Lillian Rewards loyalty program, based on a co-branded MasterCard, will be challenged to provide a comprehensive view of the retailer's customer activity.

Some experts will argue that loyalty marketing is all about recognizing and rewarding only the retailer's best customers; it is this customer segment that offers the greatest return on investment for marketing dollars. Certain retailers have designed their programs with a nod to this belief; as an example, we can look to Barnes & Noble's Reader's Advantage loyalty program. By paying $25 to join the program, customers can qualify for an additional 10% off purchases made in Barnes & Noble stores and a further 5% discount on purchases made online. Through this initiative, Barnes & Noble is hoping to identify and reward their most valuable customers.

Is this assumption correct? It may be. Yes, only customers serious about shopping with Barnes & Noble over time will find it economically worthwhile to join. Are these the company's best customers? We can assume they are, but without customer data on the other shoppers we simply do not know for sure; is there not an opportunity lost by having no knowledge of secondary shoppers who the company could possibly foster and grow?

It is highly doubtful that an experienced retailer would be comfortable making a merchandising decision based upon only a small amount of hard scan data from the POS system. The same rationale applies to recognizing and accumulating customer data on only best customers: it does not provide a comprehensive view of the retail business. Just as a product category management effort is diminished by lower scanning rates at the checkout, so too is the relevance of customer measures.

With the exception of pure web-based retailers and membership clubs, the only vehicle capable of collecting the required amounts of customer data in a mass retailing environment continues to be some type of frequent shopper or loyalty program. While a vast number of retail loyalty programs do nothing to engender relationships with their members, simply serving as electronic discount programs, properly implemented programs can be strongly effective at generating large amounts of customer data, as well as serving as a platform through which the retailer is able to alter the reward structures offered their customers, fostering customer specific communications.

It is important to remember that the primary goal in creating and launching a customer knowledge platform is to obtain customer information – a great deal of information. Given this goal, the question then becomes what cost effective incentive(s) need to be put in place to encourage customers to join and identify themselves each time they shop. The past decade has shown that far too many retailers launch such efforts without specific goals or specific long term strategies in mind.

A retailer wishing to launch a retail loyalty marketing platform should realize that the program is also part of the retail brand. The loyalty platform must reinforce the brand image of the retailer. Retailers that have done this successfully increase the power of their loyalty platform exponentially.

So what's required to assemble and launch a loyalty marketing platform in retail? In very basic terms:

- A way to identify the customer each time they shop, be it in-store or online.
- A POS system capable of capturing the customer identification and appending it to the transaction.
- The ability to collect this data from the POS system and accurately transfer it to a database; this implies some type of data network.
- The ability to identify the customer during an online transaction and collect the transaction data back to the database.
- The ability to process the data and generate actionable reports.
- The ability to transfer some level of information back to the store level.

Beyond the hardware and software requirements of assembling a loyalty platform, a retailer must look to the public face of the program; what will it look like? Looking at loyalty marketing schemes around the world in a number of retail channels we see two primary types of programs, though individual retailers often tweak these to fit their operations.

The two primary incentives used to encourage a customer to join a retailer's loyalty program, and to continue to take part in it, are price-based programs and points-based programs. Less frequently, we see air miles used as the primary incentive in loyalty programs run by retailers.

Any discussion of loyalty programs must also involve coalition-type programs. Such programs are typically created and administered by a business entity separate from the retail partners. There are examples of these types of programs around the world; for example, the airlines who partner with car rental agencies to hotels and many others. I will not dispute that there may be value for a retailer joining a coalition program from a marketing and promotional perspective, but there are inherent limitations in such a structure when pursuing a customer intelligent strategy. As one partner in a coalition program, a retailer may be constrained as to the amount and structure of customer data available. A retailer considering joining a coalition program must weigh the decision relative to their goals; coalition programs may present strong marketing opportunities but typically do not provide the data necessary for a complete customer intelligence business strategy as we are speaking of here.

Casa Sendas is Brazil's fourth largest supermarket company. Upon joining the Smart Club coalition program, Sendas' customers were able to earn points for their shopping at Sendas' stores, in addition to Shell petrol stations, a certain bank, and other retail partners, while being able to redeem points for certain gifts outlined in a catalog. While Sendas gained from a marketing perspective, they were constrained with regard to what shopping data they could access.

As with any strategic decision, many factors must be weighed in making the final choice as to the basic form of the loyalty program incentive. In the case of creating and launching a loyalty platform, the retailer must take into account the following factors:

- Competing loyalty programs in their marketplace.
- The technology already in place in the retailer's organization, and their ability to acquire additional technology.
- Any applicable legal constraints (for example, in various countries about the world it is illegal for a retailer to sell a product at two different prices to different customers, i.e., a card-based price and regular price).
- Company culture; is management willing to commit to going to market differentiating between customers? Is the company disciplined enough, and does it have the necessary human resources, to make use of the customer data gathered?
- The market position of the retailer, as seen through the eyes of consumers in the marketplace.

Carulla Vivero is Colombia's second largest food retailer, the company the result of the merger of three previously independent companies. Carulla is a very modern, upscale food retailer catering to the small middle and upper classes of Colombia. Vivero is a hypermarket, combining food with a more traditional discount store all under one roof. Merquefacil is a limited assortment, soft discount store group, featuring smaller stores located in more urban areas. At present, Merquefacil is the only member of the Carulla Vivero company without a loyalty program.

Carulla Vivero is run by Sam Azout, whose family founded Vivero, which subsequently merged with the Carulla and Merquefacil companies. Sam has assembled an impressive team of people that are focusing on many leading edge initiatives in all areas of operations. One of their most important initiatives is further development of their customer intelligence strategy. The stated goals for the company's loyalty program are to create sustainable strategic advantage, to improve patrons' shopping experience, and to build long-lasting relationships with the company's customers.

Vivero launched its loyalty program in 1998, the first loyalty program in Colombia. As with many programs we see outside the U.S., the Vivero program is points-based; customers earn one point for each Colombian peso in spending. Customers are able to track their point accumulation on the bottom of their receipt if they continue to frequent the same store; Vivero does not have a real-time data network in place to feedback point totals across all stores; customers' points totals are real-time within the individual store.

Customers can redeem their points for merchandise displayed in a gift catalog which is available in store. The gifts themselves are either available in store or are shipped to the customer's store for pick up by the customer.

As our discussions progressed during my visit to Bogota, where the company is headquartered, I learned that Carrefour was beginning to enter the Colombian market, and, in particular, had stores planned in Baranquilla, Vivero's strongest market. I also became aware that Vivero had a strong image as the low cost retailer in their markets but that Carrefour would put serious pressure on this as they are a world-class retailer known for aggressive pricing.

We can now begin to see a "disconnection" between Vivero's primary business strategy, that of being the low-cost retailer, and that of its loyalty platform, a points-based program. I say this because in many markets we have seen, a points program is, in some sense, analogous to the S&H Green Stamp type programs of yesterday.

Customers collect their stamps (or points) based upon their shopping and then redeem them for gifts. In the case of the Green Stamp programs of old, customers eventually realized that there was a cost to the retailer for such a program that reflected in higher retail prices over time; not exactly the correct impression to be delivered for a retailer seeking to maintain its low-cost image.

A far better strategy for Vivero to pursue would be to morph its points program to a price-based program; such was the plan towards the end of my visit. By shifting to a price-based loyalty platform, Vivero can now use its loyalty marketing program to reinforce its primary business strategy of being the low cost retailer. By requiring the use of its loyalty card to receive Vivero's ad specials and other marked-down items around the store, Vivero can emphasize tying together their card and low prices. In addition, they can now also reflect those savings on the customers' receipt tapes; yet again emphasizing their low prices and how much a customer will save by shopping with Vivero. The suggestion was also made that Vivero's advertising people develop a sample receipt tape so that customers understand how to read the receipt, but also to use the receipt in their marketing efforts: use the Vivero loyalty card and SAVE! The simple concept of being able to show customers their savings on the bottom of the receipt is powerful, made even more so when the competitor cannot.

This strategy will also cost-effectively help Vivero to further strengthen their identification rates, the percentage of total sales and transactions identified through their loyalty program, thus obtaining even more customer data. It also lowers their cost of collecting large amounts of customer data, as they are already incurring an expense related to their markdown, rather than adding to their cost structure with a points-based program.

The Carulla store group also was using a points-based loyalty program which had been launched approximately a year prior to my visit. Identification rates were not as substantial; Carulla was identifying approximately 60% of total sales – not enough to make further use of the data in other areas of the company. While customers could redeem their points for gift items, albeit from a much smaller collection, the primary use of points was to redeem them for lower prices on specified products throughout the store.

The Carulla stores that I visited were quite beautiful and could successfully compete in any market in the world. Customers shopping these stores were certainly not frequenting them for their prices; Carulla emphasizes high quality fresh foods in addition to dry grocery offerings. And yet the thrust behind their loyalty program was allowing customers to redeem points by lowering the selling price of products – not necessarily a strong incentive for the customer base the stores were obviously attracting.

While a points-based loyalty platform is most likely the preferred incentive scheme for the Carulla division, evolving the rewards to more lifestyle-based offerings may prove to be a more powerful attraction for their clientele. Making points redeemable for rewards such as spa treatments, dining at fine restaurants, or vacations at nicer hotels or resorts along the coasts of Colombia are more in keeping with the Carulla brand image and customer base.

The Carulla Vivero example showcases the need to coordinate a retailer's loyalty marketing program initiatives with its primary business strategy. Each should support and compliment the other, always strengthening and reinforcing the company's brand image.

Technology is also a key component of developing a retailer's loyalty marketing strategy. Obviously, should a retailer launch a points-based program, they must have in place a system of tracking and informing the customer of their point totals. Likewise, for retailers using a price-based strategy, their POS system should be capable of using a loyalty card to trigger product discounts and report the savings on the customer's receipt.

While these are obvious requirements, the need for absolute data integrity is often overlooked. One of the few areas at Carulla Vivero in need of further attention was the quality of their data networks and polling of the stores. The IT department would occasionally have trouble pulling back to the central database the entire transaction file for certain periods of time, thus causing some customers' purchases to be missed. It goes without saying that this can become a critical issue very quickly as a retailer begins to put more and more value into their loyalty program, skewing rewards to customers' shopping behavior over time.

For a different perspective, let's look to the Japanese marketplace. Retail loyalty marketing has been exploding throughout the Japanese retail scene since the late 1990s. Commonly referred to as FSP (Frequent Shopper Program), most Japanese retailers have studied the concept for quite some time, many of them making numerous trips to the U.S. and Europe to study programs in action.

During my initial visits there, I observed many retailers operating points programs, the vast majority of which were simply promotional gimmicks.

Customers would earn points for their shopping, the points in turn being redeemed for certain rewards. These retailers were not capturing detailed customer data; in fact, many of them were not even capturing basic contact data such as name and address.

There appeared to be a very strong aversion to a price-based scheme as is typically operated in the U.S. markets. Various retailers strongly felt that a price-based loyalty scheme would not be accepted by their customers. During this time, several world-class retailers were beginning to move into the Japanese market, specifically, Costco and Carrefour, with Tesco and Wal-Mart not far behind. Seeing this, we realized that heightened price competition would not be far behind.

After much discussion, a struggling multi-store supermarket chain located outside Tokyo decided to launch a price-based scheme. The company launched very aggressively, moving all price reductions (advertised specials, etc.) to requiring their FSP card within a matter of weeks. Following the strategy in the Vivero example, this retailer emphasized the savings available to customers joining and using their loyalty card, using this tactic to reinforce their low-price image.

This Japanese retailer was capturing over 80% of all sales through their loyalty card within two weeks of launch (the rates continuing to climb from that point). Of even more importance, their total sales began accelerating very quickly and gross profit margins began climbing. Within the first year, as the retailer began recognizing and rewarding their higher spending customers, the supermarket company was in turn the recipient of substantial sales and profit gains.

As I hope these examples convey, retailers hoping to succeed in this arena must give careful thought and study to the type of loyalty platform they wish to assemble and the competitive activities in their marketplace. Fresh, original thinking wins the day; me-too offerings simply do not produce strong results.

During a visit to Hawaii I was able to visit several supermarket retailers on the island of Oahu, each with a retail loyalty program, but each nearly a mirror-image of the others.

Safeway operates a division of supermarkets in the islands. The stores do a good job of promoting their Safeway Club frequent shopper card, and the card is prominently featured in their ad flyers. As found in many U.S. supermarket programs, Safeway requires their card for any shopper to receive discounts on advertised products. In addition, for each $250 in accumulated purchases, a customer can earn a 5% discount certificate to be used on a future shopping trip.

Foodland is a small chain of supermarkets also located on Oahu. They have offered their Maika'i program for several years now, and extend several benefits to their members. The first benefit, like Safeway, is receiving the discounts on their advertised and specially marked products around the store. In addition, for every dollar in spending customers earn one point; for every 250 points collected over time, customers can earn a 5% discount certificate to be used on a future shopping trip, or the customer can choose to receive 250 AlohaPass miles on Aloha airlines, good for inter-island travel.

Times Supermarkets is also headquartered on Oahu; formerly owned by a local family, Times has since been acquired by a California-based supermarket company. At the time of my visit, Times offered their Royal Card loyalty program, providing similar benefits to the cardholders; specifically, discounts on their advertised items and also the ability to earn a 5% discount certificate or air miles, albeit on an alternative Hawaiian airline.

So here are three supermarket companies operating in the same market, each with a loyalty program, and all providing nearly identical benefits. There was not enough evident differentiation between the programs to enable one program to stand out, offering demonstrably superior benefits or even unique operations.

What would be suggested in this scenario? While the Safeway program and the Times Supermarket company were similar in that each required a $250 spend to qualify for the 5% discount certificate, Foodland was basing their program on points (albeit one point for each dollar in spending). But Foodland could have conceivably leveraged their points program into a much stronger offering.

The first tactic involves moving away from making every deal product available at a discount with the Maika'i card, instead making some of these products available at regular price but with the opportunity for the customer to earn bonus points or double points when purchasing the specified products, thus substituting points for markdown expense which will bolster margins. Going further, Foodland should have taken advantage of its position as a locally owned company enjoying a strong reputation to begin building a network of non-competing merchants – video stores, service stations, restaurants, etc. – which would also accept their Maika'i card and award the customer additional points.

In this manner, Foodland could begin to clearly differentiate their program as being points-based, providing the customer opportunity to earn points, and the related benefits, for their shopping at a number of other retail and service providers around the island.

4) It's All About the Customer!

Time and again in articles and news stories deriding retail loyalty programs is the focus on comparing product prices with non-card competitors, no word mentioned of the long term rewards and values enjoyed by a retailer's regular shoppers. This is what loyalty programs are all about – rewarding the regular shoppers with increased values. Such news stories are only relating half the story, neglecting the values received by the regular customers, and forgetting to mention that the regular shoppers at non-card retailers are subsidizing the deal-seeking consumers.

Retail companies, to be successful with a long term strategy of building and using customer knowledge, must deliver real value to their participating customers. And yet we continue to see a vast number of retail companies around the world position their loyalty platforms or CRM initiatives as price discounting schemes or public relations efforts aimed at boosting sales.

As the airline companies make free tickets and upgrades ever harder to get, their frequent flyer programs are rapidly losing luster, sending previously loyal passengers in search of the lowest airfares. Many flyers have become disenfranchised, maintaining that the airline loyalty programs no longer deliver value.

With some exceptions, larger retail companies have found delivering true value to certain customers exceedingly difficult to carry out in practice. In many cases, these companies focus only on delivering more discounts to their customers, often by negotiating with their suppliers for more deals. This focus comes from the product myopic vision that large companies suffer from. They have lost sight of the idea that value to a customer can mean many things; value does not necessarily have to be measured in dollars.

Smaller retail companies seem to possess an innate sense of the value of customer information and how it can be used to further build the relationship they have with their patrons. These are the companies we see acting as the true entrepreneurs they are, creatively bestowing services and privileges upon their more valuable customers. Realizing they cannot win price-based competition, these smaller retailers have expanded the value equation to include customer recognition and the shopping experience.

Don Lemp, third generation proprietor of M. Lemp Jewelers in Syracuse, New York, understands the value of building customer relationships. He relates the story of a young man from New York City (the fourth generation of his family to shop with Lemp Jewelers), who traveled to Syracuse to purchase his wedding bands, making a sizeable purchase. Lemp has instilled the importance of customer loyalty and customer retention in his organization, encouraging each associate to develop a relationship with their customers.

Gary Friedlander and his team at Rice Epicurean Markets regularly receive thank-you cards and e-mail messages from customers thanking the company for their acknowledgement of them as valued patrons.

One M&M Meat Shops franchisee discovered that one of his best customers drives over 100 miles several times per month to shop at the store, all because the customer loves being acknowledged as a best customer.

Green Hills has received notes, letters, and thank-you cards from many customers over the years thanking the store for the free holiday turkeys and other gifts bestowed upon regular shoppers. One memorable older customer even sends a holiday card each year, enclosing $10 to be used for thanking employees.

Yes, these examples, and countless others from stores around the world, are from smaller companies, not the large, faceless retail behemoths. But larger retail companies can push in this direction by driving the understanding and use of customer information down to the store and even departmental level. Going further, by tying some portion of the store's management team's financial incentives to reflect customer measures, like the retention of Tier 1 customers, the company will begin to embed the importance and value of customer knowledge into their companies.

Bashas', a Phoenix, Arizona supermarket chain, issues a store report card every quarter to each of its stores. Christie Frazier-Coleman, VP of Sales Promotion and Customer Loyalty, divides the customers of each store into three segments, showing a trend within each segment from preceding quarters. Store managers are now being held to new measures of performance: customer-based measures of performance.[6]

Consumers are starving for attention. Many retail companies today are more concerned with costs and logistics, processing customers through their stores and checkout lines like cattle. While customer data and the resulting analyses, reporting, and economics are vitally important, the essential goal is to focus on the customer. Customer knowledge provides a unique opportunity for a retail company to truly develop and become responsible for relationships with their customers.

CUSTOMER INTELLIGENT STRATEGY IN ACTION

As the following stories highlight, retailers relying on product-based business models face ever increasing hurdles which they must surmount to survive, let alone thrive. From supermarkets to discounters and bookstores to department stores, every retailer in every retail sector is presented with challenges from inside and outside their traditional channel, threatening sales and margins.

Those pioneers who have embarked upon understanding and using customer knowledge to solidify and improve their businesses understand that they must seek advantage in altering the rules of engagement. Product-based business strategies alone are no longer enough to ensure success.

Following are three case studies, each focusing on a retail company and how it is making use of a customer intelligent strategy. We shall examine in detail the evolution of M&M Meat Shops' efforts at gathering and using customer data, how Rice Epicurean Markets uses customer information to defend itself against competitive interlopers, and how Green Hills is creating synergy between its product and customer strategies.

Lastly, we shall observe and evaluate one of the larger retail battles being waged: that between the Kroger Company and Wal-Mart. We will close with a look at the scene in Japan where we see customer-focused business strategies playing out on a large scale.

M&M Meat Shops

While grilling steaks at a backyard barbecue over two decades ago, Mac Voisin grew frustrated with the quality of the steaks that had been purchased from a local supermarket. Realizing that fine steakhouses could offer a tender, flavorful steak for every meal, Mac wondered why people couldn't purchase the same restaurant quality steaks to prepare at home. He was determined to capitalize on what he saw as an opportunity.

Beginning with one store in Kitchener, Ontario, where M&M Meat Shops is headquartered, Mac began purchasing food service products which he repackaged for sale to the consumer. With adjustments to the food preparation directions and a great deal of customer education, Mac was on to something. Mac and his partner began franchising other M&M Meat Shops stores and the company began to grow. Today M&M Meat Shops is one of Canada's largest franchise companies with stores throughout the country.

As the company grew, and locating sites for new stores became increasingly important, Greg Voisin, Mac's brother, came aboard. In charge of new franchises, Greg is responsible for the marketing studies and demographic analysis needed to identify strong potential locations. M&M Meat Shops continues to open stores at a strong pace across the country of Canada. Mac continued to build a strong management team by bringing in other experienced people such as James Petrozzi, formerly an executive with Schneiders, Canada's largest meat-packing house. As Chief Operating Officer, James brought a lifetime of experience with not only products but also operations to the growing M&M Meat Shops organization.

When M&M Meat Shops began business in 1980 their product offering was unique; self-branded frozen food items, individually packaged and portion controlled, and sold only in M&M shops. Until that time, the idea of frozen boxed meats had not yet taken hold; consumers were accustomed to purchasing their meat fresh from the local butcher or supermarket. Today, M&M Meat Shops remains a niche retailer, selling only a few hundred frozen food products. Their stores are typically 1,500 square feet in size and located in strip plazas, providing local convenience for customers while enabling the company to control lease costs.

What is most unique about the stores is perhaps best described by their slogan: "Hundreds of meal ideas. One aisle". Walking into an M&M Meat Shops store, the customer will encounter on the right hand side of the store a smaller self-service frozen food case; the primary product display area is on the left, the frozen boxed products on display behind glass doors set into the large walk-in freezer. A sales clerk, known as a product consultant, assists the customer with their purchase, selecting the requested product from the frozen display.

M&M Meat Shops' original business strategy was a classic product-based business model. The products (at the time) were unique in the marketplace, were only available at M&M Meat Shops, were retailer-branded, and offered good margins. The quality of product was good but not so high as to make the price points unreasonable. Customer interaction was stressed as educating consumers as to the products and preparation was, and is, critical to success. But early on, M&M Meat Shops went to market by making its products the center of attention.

For some years, M&M Meat Shops quietly went about building their business as a niche retail channel, far different than traditional mainstream supermarkets. Having no direct competition, the company's unique product offering and mix was the basis for much of their early success. In a real sense, M&M Meat Shops was building a very successful business off the radar screen of the mainline supermarket companies. But few competitive positions are secure forever.

Up the road in Toronto is the headquarters of Loblaws, Canada's largest supermarket company, with stores coast to coast and annual sales in excess of CDN$20 billion, giving the company approximately 30% of Canadian supermarket sales. Loblaws is held in high regard by those in the industry, an innovator and pioneer in many areas of food retailing, particularly with regard to private label goods.

Starting in the late 1980s, Loblaws began to build their President's Choice line of private label products. Now one of the premier private label programs in food retailing, Loblaws systematically targeted one product category after another in building their brand. It was not long before M&M Meat Shops attracted their attention. As any retailer knows, it is very difficult to keep secrets for long in the trade. Word began to spread of the success of M&M Meat Shops' business and the volume of products that they were selling company-wide.

For the first time, M&M Meat Shops had direct competition at the heart of their product-based business strategy and model; much larger competitors threatening more aggressive price points and lower profit margins on similar products.

The management team of M&M Meat Shops decided to maintain their focus on quality products in the face of this competition, knowing that lowering quality to match competitive price points would be a losing strategy when confronting the major supermarket companies, companies much larger than themselves. Instead they would stress their customer service, thus making this attribute of their business model much more critical to the shopping experience they offered consumers. They would develop their customer service function into a strategic asset, making it a vital part of how they go to market and of their business strategy.

As mentioned earlier, a customer wishing to purchase products must interact with an M&M Meat Shops product consultant. The product consultant will select the requested item from the freezer, open the box for inspection and explain the unique attributes of the product. While speaking with the customer, the product consultant will also make suggestions about other products, perhaps complimentary items or frozen desserts.

Contrast this business model with supermarkets and club stores; M&M Meat Shops' direct competition. The supermarket industry has achieved significant gains in operating efficiencies in large part by encouraging the consumer to do much of the work. Consider a typical visit to a modern supermarket; parking their vehicle, a customer enters the store, perhaps selecting a trolley or basket in which to put their purchases. Proceeding around the store, the customer encounters a vast array of products, most of which are available in a self-service setting so that they can make their own selections at their own pace. Having made their selections, the customer then proceeds to the check-out, where increasingly patrons have the choice of an automated self-checkout system, paying for their purchases with either a credit or debit card. Bagging their groceries, the customer then departs the store... without ever having to speak to any store personnel.

Though the supermarket sells many products similar to the frozen boxed meats and other items offered by M&M Meat Shops, the customer has an entirely different shopping experience.

The updated M&M Meat Shops business model is one of customer service; the company sees this service-based shopping experience as a strategic advantage. A customer cannot purchase anything at M&M Meat Shops without interacting with the staff. While some consumers may prefer the anonymity of shopping in a large store, many people do indeed value speaking with another human being and doing business with an establishment where they feel recognized and valued as a customer.

So here we have a large retail business, with several hundred stores, which is dependent upon customer service and customer-staff interaction. How does one measure the effectiveness of a customer-based business strategy? By developing and using customer-based business measures.

Chris Styan brought with him a strong background in direct marketing when he joined M&M Meat Shops as Director of Marketing in the late 1980s. Convinced he could bring the principles of direct marketing to a retail setting, Chris has been focused on developing the use of customer information within the company for much of the past decade.

M&M Meat Shops' first attempt at developing a customer focus took place in the early 1990s. At that time, only a handful of retail companies around the world had invested in the technologies to allow them to begin capturing great amounts of customer data through their POS systems. Acknowledging that creating such a technological infrastructure would be a stretch for the company at that time, M&M Meat Shops instead joined a coalition loyalty program led by Zellers, a Canadian discount department store chain.

Consumers participating in Club Z, Zellers' loyalty program, had the ability to earn points based upon their shopping at any of the participating retail partners, such as M&M Meat Shops. But, as with many coalition programs about the world, the benefits often primarily accrue to the lead company running the program. Participating retail merchants must pay for the points awarded to their customers, yet have limited ability to access and make use of detailed customer information.

After several years it became apparent that this first effort at developing a customer focus was failing at M&M Meat Shops. The stores were burdened with the high costs of awarding points but did not realize any gain from joining the coalition. The program was terminated, allowing M&M Meat Shops to return its focus to its own operations.

The company made its next attempt at developing a loyalty program by assembling and launching a pilot program in one of its regions. The Plus program, brought to market in the mid 1990's, proved to Styan that the company could indeed get customers to sign up for a loyalty program and begin collecting data. This pilot was successful enough to encourage M&M Meat Shops to proceed with a more intensive effort, developing a revised program to be rolled out nationally.

As Pegi Klein-Weber, Marketing Manager for M&M Meat Shops, explained it to me: "The goal of the MAX program was to identify and focus on best customers. Having identified them, M&M Meat Shops, along with the franchisees, would mail special offers to them and otherwise attempt to recognize and reward these valuable customers so as to maintain them."

M&M Meat Shops' goal was correct: recognize, reward, and retain the highest value customers... but there were some difficulties along the way. The program was structured so that each of the stores participating in the trial was provided MAX loyalty cards and applications. Each store was encouraged to only sign up their best customers for the MAX program. I asked Pegi how they defined a Best Customer, her response being a customer spending approximately CDN$40 or more in a single transaction. This number was derived from focus group and customer survey information M&M Meat Shops had gathered.

Getting out into the stores to see and understand how this operated in a real-world situation reinforced my apprehension for pursuing a best customer strategy to the exclusion of a more comprehensive effort at gathering customer data.

I asked each of the store franchisees I met how they decided to invite certain customers to sign up for the MAX program; without fail, I received a different answer each time. In one case, the franchisee was signing up every customer they could regardless of spending; in another store, the franchisee would only offer to sign up customers he knew had spent hundreds of dollars with him. The telling fact here is that there was no consistency between stores in how customers were signed up, yet all customers signed up were to be treated as best customers, regardless of spending. In some cases, M&M Meat Shops would be recognizing and rewarding customers who had spent a great deal of money; in other cases, they'd be rewarding only very occasional, low value customers. And, in many stores, they would simply be missing many of the most valuable customers because the franchisee didn't bother to invite them into the program!

Discussions as to where the program was heading ensued. Initial meetings were focused upon helping the top management team develop an understanding of the differences, both philosophically and operationally, between conventional loyalty marketing (such as the early MAX program was) and a more comprehensive customer intelligence strategy. In pursuing this strategy, identifying only supposed "best customers" would no longer be enough; Styan's goal was to make M&M Meat Shops a world-class practitioner of customer intelligence.

This change in perspective is critical. As a company moves from a best customer view to a comprehensive view afforded by enormous amounts of customer data, they are fundamentally moving from a marketing initiative to a long term business strategy involving the entire company.

Once the decision had been made to pursue a comprehensive customer strategy at M&M Meat Shops, attention turned to information systems.

When M&M Meat Shops had first rolled out their early MAX loyalty program they used a third party database services provider to host their customer data; the service provider in turn provided store level reports and was responsible for direct mail programs initiated by the head office. Further research brought to light several areas which were problematic for the early MAX loyalty platform.

The first issue encountered was that M&M Meat Shops had no way of quickly assessing the level of information gathering through the MAX program; there was no way to easily measure the percentage of total sales and transactions being identified. This basic measure continues to offer the strongest assessment of a retailer's commitment to customer intelligence. Further, there were significant operational issues that had already begun to degrade the value of the program and reporting issues that would have grown far worse with time. For example, when a new customer was signed up for the MAX program, the data services company was to mail out a new customer greeting and offer; it was discovered that such offers were going out to new customers several months after their initial store visit. Such a lag between behavior and reward is harmful, potentially alienating customers who would perceive M&M Meat Shops as poorly organized.

The next issue arising from the database system related to the type of reporting provided both the head office staff and the store franchisees. The service provider did direct mail work and other targeted offers for publications and other retail clients. Their usual analytical work involved segmentation schemes using recency, frequency, and spending, a method commonly used in traditional database work for mail order publications. While more appropriate customer reporting could have been developed for M&M Meat Shops, it was not deemed cost effective. Furthermore, there were issues related to data cleansing, ensuring the accuracy of customer contact information. All told, the decision was made to look for other solutions to support the MAX loyalty platform.

After much research and many meetings, it was decided that M&M Meat Shops would purchase a turnkey solution; the primary work involved mapping the data feed from the POS transaction files to the database. The system would be located in the MIS department of M&M Meat Shops. This solution allowed the company to move quickly at controlled cost to further develop their information gathering capabilities and yet provide the marketing department campaign management and customer analytics. It was understood that over time, as the MAX program continued to evolve and grow, that the systems supporting it would need to do the same.

With the database system in place, attention was turned to loading data into it, both customer contact data and sales data. The sales data was relatively straightforward, making sure that information was captured properly and that all required data, item sales, item costs, and customer discounts, were captured at the POS. Obtaining and loading accurate customer contact data was another matter.

Many of the individual M&M Meat Shops stores had built their own customer databases using functionality available in their store level POS systems. The outside service M&M Meat Shops originally used to host the early MAX program had tried to import data from all these individual store databases to create a centralized master database. It was found that the same customer could appear in different stores' databases, the result of cross shopping.

Adding to the complexity, the same customer could be entered in multiple store level databases but with a slight difference in name spelling or address, appearing as two distinct customers when in reality it was the same person. As the central database grew, the quality of the contact data began to deteriorate. This illustrates an important point: in any retail customer intelligence effort there can be only one source of data, one "bible" if you will, that must always be the true source of information. There was no way that M&M Meat Shops could maintain accuracy of customer contact data when assimilating data drawn from over 300 individual stores, each of whom built its database to track different information, storing it in different fields.

As customers had signed up for the program in the past, the completed applications were mailed to the outside data provider; this was cause for some of the processing delays related to new customer offers. Questions soon arose as to how customer contact data would be entered in a timely, cost effective manner as M&M Meat Shops brought their database capability in-house.

John Newell, Director of MIS for M&M Meat Shops, helped to craft an innovative yet deceptively simple solution to the dilemma. The answer was the creation of a website created by M&M Meat Shops for the maintenance of customer contact data. An individual store would collect their completed customer applications and, on a regular basis, enter the information into the website database. While putting some of the labor burden on the stores, this process also helped ensure more accurate data, local people being much more knowledgeable of street addresses, phone numbers, etc. than someone keypunching data a few thousand kilometers away.

This website has continued to provide additional functionality for the store owners in that they can enter new customer contact data, link new card numbers to lost cards, add and delete customers, and do some basic search functions on their customers. Furthermore, the data from the website is polled each day and loaded into the central database regularly. Each week an export file containing the contact data for any and every customer having shopped at an individual store or in any stores in the region is downloaded into each store's POS database each week, thus keeping the store's information current.

M&M Meats Shops data flow

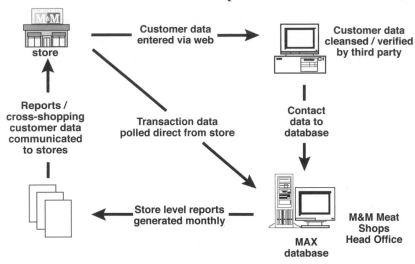

store

Customer data
entered via web

Customer data
cleansed / verified
by third party

Reports /
cross-shopping
customer data
communicated
to stores

Transaction data
polled direct from store

Contact
data to
database

Store level reports
generated monthly

MAX
database

M&M Meat
Shops
Head Office

In the case of M&M Meat Shops we were able to make one of the unique characteristics of their POS system work in their favor. Franchisees have the capability to build their own database within their POS system. By making use of this capability at store level, customers can simply provide their telephone number if they have forgotten their MAX card. The clerk enters the phone number, by which the computer locates the customer in the store's database and positively identifies the customer, appending the customer's MAX number to the transaction.

A word of caution: what allows M&M Meat Shops to use a customer's phone number as a customer identifier is the fact that their system looks up the customer so that the clerk can positively verify that it is indeed him or her. Some retailers in the past have tried to use a customer phone number as an identification number, blindly inputting the number the customer gives them. Without positively verifying the that number is that of the customer, the retailer soon finds that their database is corrupted.

The importance of gathering accurate customer data at the store level cannot be stressed enough. M&M Meat Shops has been strongly disciplined to execute processes to insure the integrity of their information going forward. For example, when a customer requests a MAX card, the clerk will ask if they are indeed a new customer to M&M Meat Shops or if they need a replacement card, the customer having lost theirs. What may seem a minor point becomes critically important later when viewing and taking action on new customers. At M&M Meat Shops, new customers are truly new; replacement cards or additional household cards are linked within the database to the other existing cards (this is again done through the internal portal described earlier).

Contrast this practice with a regional supermarket chain in the U.S. who is not as disciplined. In this company, new loyalty cards are frequently issued to customers requesting one without asking the relevant information: are they truly a new customer or is it a replacement or additional card? In this case, the retailer has attempted to work with new customer data, but the "new customer" numbers are highly inflated because many of the new cards issued are in fact replacement cards for existing customers. This retailer is not measuring new customer behavior; they are measuring existing customer shopping behavior, believing it to be new customers. The loyalty group within this retailer produces analysis and reporting relative to new customers and marketing programs directed to them, much of it based on erroneous data.

The error in the data compounds for each customer added and each day that passes. The retailer is no longer able to view, analyze, or take action on accurate information. Further, the company begins to add to their costs (marketing to new customers who do not exist) and communicates to customers that they are not well organized. Imagine a customer receiving a new customer mailing (based on a replacement card viewed by the company as "new") concomitant with receiving a lost customer mailing (based on the lost card no longer being used).

With the systems in place, M&M Meat Shops could give attention to turning up the dial on gathering customer sales information. Multiple layers of incentives were created to encourage customers to join the MAX program and to use their cards each time they shopped, thus identifying themselves.

Sweepstakes

M&M Meat Shops runs a sweepstakes contest each month, awarding free product prizes to 10 customers at each store. Customers receive an entry automatically each time they used their MAX card. In addition, M&M Meat

Shops runs national sweepstakes contests on a regular basis throughout the year with much larger prizes; vacations to Disney, barbecue grills, etc.

Many retailers have found sweepstakes to be a cost effective way to create interest in their loyalty platforms, encouraging customers to join and use their card each time they shop.

Prices

At re-launch of the MAX program, M&M Meat Shops began tying several items in the ad flyer to the MAX card, customers only able to receive the special pricing by using their card. Initially these MAX items were found on inside pages of the company's ad flyer, but as MAX membership grew, these products were moved to the front page and made even stronger. The special prices and savings for MAX members were further reinforced when the company began reporting MAX savings on customers' receipt tapes.

The primary purpose of a price-based (or even a points-based) platform is to provide an everyday incentive encouraging customers to take part. While sweepstakes and threshold programs can be powerful incentives in their own right, they are not ongoing, usually limited to specific time periods.

Threshold Programs

Within three months of launch, M&M Meat Shops rolled out their first reward program, encouraging customers to do more shopping with the company over time. The first threshold program rewarded those customers achieving a CDN$250 or CDN$350 threshold a 10% or 20% savings certificate respectively, the certificate good for use on a future shopping trip to M&M Meat Shops. Subsequent programs have used electric knives, coolers, and a free turkey for the holiday.

Threshold programs serve three important purposes:
1) Threshold programs create incentive for customers to join and participate in a retailer's loyalty platform.
2) Properly executed, threshold programs create strong incentive for customers to centralize their purchasing with a retailer so as to qualify for the reward.
3) Such programs offer one method for a company to begin skewing its marketing expenditures to higher spending customers.

At M&M Meat Shops, during the first year of the intensified MAX program, the foremost goal of threshold programs was to create additional incentives for customers to join and use their cards. Any benefits derived from customers centralizing their purchasing (possibly increasing sales) and skewing values to higher spending customers (possibly raising margins) was considered secondary.

These are important points. M&M Meat Shops realized that this was a long term business strategy; they must invest in building a rich repository of customer data. Certainly, as the MAX program evolves, some of these incentives will be directly evaluated as to their efficacy in changing customer shopping behavior and return on investment for the company. Too many retail companies launch loyalty programs looking for a "quick fix", an immediate gain in sales and/or profitability. In those companies that do experience a rapid gain in sales activity, it is typically the case that they have created a great deal of promotion around their program, not because they have an effective loyalty program.

A regional retail company I am familiar with launched its loyalty program to great fanfare, offering heavily discounted products tied to their frequent shopper card in addition to sweepstakes. Management was excited to report strong sales gains resulting from the launch. These gains were made more impressive due to the fact the company had capitalized all its promotional expenses (and extra discounting) related to the card launch, for the most part moving the expenses off their operating profit and loss statements. Accounting propriety aside, this company did not understand the long term value of gathering, understanding, and using customer information. As do many retailers, they were looking for the "silver bullet".

All told, the incentives put in place by M&M Meat Shops began to take effect, and identification levels (the percentage of sales and transactions identified to customers) for the MAX program began to climb. Within three months of launch, M&M Meat Shops as a company was identifying over 80% of total sales back to individual customers, with a number of individual stores identifying over 90%. Within six months, the total company was identifying 90% of total sales, with a majority of stores over this threshold. Early on, having no appreciable history of data to analyze, the most important measure for a retailer to watch is their levels of identification. Each week, reports were produced showing the MAX identification levels for each individual store, rolled up by region, and then total company. Great effort was devoted by both head office and the regional support teams to get each store on board and identifying strong levels of total sales through MAX.

The first year of the revitalized MAX program was spent driving customer participation so as to develop a strong foundation of customer information upon which to build. Chris Styan and his team have done an exemplary job of redirecting a substantial portion of the company's past mass marketing expenditures to support the MAX program and customer-focused marketing. Through judicious planning and creative scheduling, his team was able to decrease budgeted spending on mass media communications and certain direct mail promotions, instead directing those monies to supporting their threshold reward programs and other MAX-based activities. By doing so, the company is able to reflect a great portion of their increased customer spending and margin on their bottom line.

Within the first year, as customer information began to accumulate, M&M Meat Shops Head Office began encouraging the store owners to focus on recognizing their best customers. One of the first such efforts involved suggesting that the store owners hand-deliver a rose bouquet to their best customers on Valentine's Day. While many stores thought this a bit much, those owners that followed through were met by an overwhelming response from their customers. The word of mouth developed by such exorbitant recognition of customers is invaluable.

These activities have been continued through a focused attempt to recognize each store's best customers several times during the year, including such gifts as fine chocolates or steak knives. M&M Meat Shops' focus and attention to developing relationships with its customers are second to none. This focus was further reinforced by the discovery that its top tier of patrons represented a lifetime value of over fifty times that of lower tier customers. Such findings helped bring home the importance of customer information to everyone in the M&M Meat Shops organization.

Through its MAX customer knowledge platform, M&M Meat Shops is able to glean incredible insight into its customers' shopping behavior and has developed key business measures that are made available on a regular basis to each individual store. Such reporting has been incorporated into the financial and management reporting systems used by M&M Meat Shops throughout the company, from Head Office to the Regional Offices, and to the individual store level.

These monthly reports provide for each store the composition of the store's customer base, allowing the franchisee to know how many new customers his/her store is attracting each month, the number of regular, existing customers, and the number of customers that have lapsed. Going even deeper, each store is provided a Customer Tier report which segments the customers each month into different value streams, thus allowing the proprietor to truly understand where his/her sales and profits are originating. By measuring and tracking the retention of their different customer segments, M&M Meat Shops' operators now have invaluable feedback as to the quality of their customer service and operations.

M&M Meat Shops is also capitalizing on its organizational structure to make use of benchmarking through the development of store scorecards, comparing individual stores' performance with other stores in the region or province. Field Consultants, each responsible for a group of stores, review this report with each store on a quarterly basis, further reinforcing the company's focus on gathering, understanding, and using detailed customer information.

The knowledge provided by reports such as these is made powerful because it is based upon M&M Meat Shops' identification of tremendous levels of their total sales through the MAX program; M&M Meat Shops is world-class in this regard, identifying 90% of total sales across the company week in and week out. Finally having over a year and a quarter's worth of high levels of customer data provides for benchmarking, allowing management to compare the composition of their customer base to prior-year periods, constantly measuring customer retention.

Quarterly Store Benchmarking Report

	Store # _____			Comparison	
	This Year	Last Year	% Change	Region Index	Company Index
% of Total Sales Identified via MAX					
Total Sales $ Sales Detail *Tier 1 (% of total)* *Tier 2 (% of total)* *Tier 3 (% of total)* *Tier 4 (% of total)* *Unidentified*					
Gross Margin %					
Total Customer Households # Household Detail *Tier 1 (% of total)* *Tier 2 (% of total)* *Tier 3 (% of total)* *Tier 4 (% of total)*					
Customer Retention — All Customers Retention Detail *Tier 1* *Tier 2* *Tier 3* *Tier 4*					
Shopping Frequency (VPM) Average Frequency Detail *Tier 1* *Tier 2* *Tier 3* *Tier 4*					

Practitioners of customer intelligent retailing come to view their strategy as a journey, each week bringing new discoveries in customer shopping behavior. As companies build their history of customer information they find that, along with knowledge, come more questions.

Joan Hergott, Marketing Systems Supervisor for M&M Meat Shops, is responsible for overseeing the reporting and analysis done from the MAX database. One of her projects is the production of store level best customer lists that are used by the stores in recognizing their most valued shoppers. As the MAX program evolved into its second year, and Joan had that much more customer information to work with, she began to question how she should be defining Best Customers.

During the first year of the MAX program, the company used straightforward definitions for acknowledging its most valuable customers. For example, by generating a list of the ten highest spending customers during a period of time for each store, Joan was able to provide the franchisees with easily understood information. But as the program moved into its second year, it appeared that such segmentations were no longer ideal.

As historical data grew, we began to study customer retention from month to month, quarter to quarter, and year to year. This type of analysis began to show the ebb and flow of customers through the company's stores. Joan noticed that customers that may be amongst the highest spending in one quarter may not have been classified as such in prior or subsequent periods.

This discovery leads us back to a discussion — one continuing today amongst leading retailers the world over — as to how to define a Best Customer. Is it a person who is simply high spending over a certain time period? Is it someone who shops regularly throughout the year, but perhaps is not amongst the highest spending customers within any given time frame? In other retail settings, is it someone who shops multiple departments or categories within a store? How about a customer shopping consistently over years of time, but never qualifying as a high spending customer? What about the profitability of the customer?

As one can begin to understand, there are no simple answers. From a marketing perspective, there is as much validity to qualifying a best customer by spending as there is based upon regular shopping over years of time.

Chris Styan and his team are pushing ahead, creating a definition that incorporates many of the factors mentioned, yet one that can be easily understood as it is communicated through the company. Many times the best method of segmentation is dependent upon the ultimate use for which it is intended. Best Customers can be defined in any number of ways, the most appropriate dependent upon what the information is to be used for and what the goals are for the program.

Today, the M&M Meat Shops Company consists of more than 350 franchise stores stretching across Canada. The challenges associated with driving an integrated retailing strategy through such a company structure are immense. In a sense, each of the franchisees must be convinced of the importance of gathering, understanding, and use of customer data. Mac and his team meet with all the stores by region twice a year. In addition, a company-wide convention is held annually. Other communications are maintained on a frequent basis via faxed and e-mailed correspondence. Each of these venues has played a role in establishing and furthering M&M Meat Shops' customer knowledge business strategy. M&M Meat Shops provides a textbook example of the importance of management commitment.

The top management team was involved in the planning and execution of their MAX loyalty platform from the start. Prior to taking the program to their franchisees, a detailed plan was developed for the first two years of operation. Understanding that commitment at the top is critical in the success of any retailer's loyalty platform; Mac Voisin personally discussed and committed the company to their course of action. Through a combination of selling the program on its merits and providing a thorough education to each of the store owners as to the long term benefits of the plan and what could be done with customer data, and providing incentives to the stores to drive to the desired 90% identification level, and disincentives to those stores more reluctant to take part, management made clear its commitment to this as a key business strategy at every turn.

I think it is worthwhile to note that the M&M Meat Shops organization, though it is composed of several hundred individual stores owned by independent franchisees, is a more cohesive organization than many typical corporate retail organizations of similar or even smaller size. While an argument could be made that the franchisees are self-motivated due to their financial involvement to take advantage of new business tools, a great deal can be learned from M&M Meat Shops relative to the need for informing, educating, and explaining to all associates the reasons why a certain strategy is important to the company.

According to Mac, using customer information gathered through the MAX program "allows us to get up-close and personal with our customers — capitalizing on our store environment to develop relationships with our customers, unlike larger stores." The M&M Meat Shops team is well on the way to accomplishing their goal of making the company a global leader in customer intelligence.

Rice Epicurean Markets

Rice Epicurean Markets has long catered to the well-to-do of the Houston, Texas, market by providing high quality fresh foods and a wide assortment of specialty and gourmet products. Gary Friedlander, President of Rice Epicurean, realized that as the competitive situation in the Houston market worsened, he might not be able to assume that their existing customer base would remain loyal. This realization led to the launch of their Experience Card customer knowledge platform in the Fall of 2000.

Friedlander had studied loyalty marketing for several years until finally deciding to make the leap. Though the company had committed to a certain POS platform and software package, they had not yet decided on a database system or other details regarding their program. Gary and I spent a great deal of time discussing Rice's customer base, their marketing, and the form their proposed loyalty program should take.

I regularly heard from members of the management team during my visits that customers did not shop at Rice for their prices; indeed, the stores are filled with a wide variety of specialty offerings in addition to basic grocery products. Yet there seemed to be a lapse between what the management group believed was motivating their customer base (high quality foods, good service), and their advertising. Rice was running item and price-based advertising in the Houston newspapers twice each week, regularly matching the lowest prices in the market on soda and other volume items.

We vacillated between launching a points-based program and a price-based program for quite some time. The final decision was to use a price-based program for several reasons. First, although the Rice management team was claiming that their prices were not motivating their customers, the team was spending an inordinate amount of time each week preparing and deliberating over the items and prices to be advertised. A price-based strategy would be more effective in that type of advertising environment.

Additionally, the technologies required were an important factor in the decision making process. The POS systems that had been committed to by the company were capable of supporting a price-based loyalty scheme; each time the customer scanned their loyalty card it would trigger the discount on products offered at a below-regular retail price and would report the card-based savings on the bottom of the transaction receipt to the customer.

The technology to operate an effective points-based program can be daunting. Ideally, the retailer's technology systems should be able to support point-earning schemes beyond a basic one point for one dollar spent basis. Capabilities such as offering bonus points when purchasing certain products, or enabling double point days are very important in attempting to skew customer behavior. Further, the retailer should maintain a real-time network between all stores and the central database so that customers can shop several stores and yet see their current points balance from whatever store they currently shop.

Additionally, the retailer must commit to developing the communication channels required to maximize the value of a points-based program. Reflecting a customer's point totals on the bottom of the receipt is basic; can the customer access their total through the retailer's website? How about through a kiosk in the store? Or by telephone, using a toll-free number and an interactive voice response system? Through statements e-mailed to the customer each month? Or the points total sent via e-mail to the customer's mobile phone when they're near the store entrance? Technology today is an asset and a strategic weapon.

These types of technologies were beyond Rice's capabilities at the time. Rice Epicurean Markets may have found it challenging, due to their relatively small size, to assemble appropriate rewards to be used with a points program. Based upon their view of their customer base, earning points to redeem for a new coffee maker was simply not going to do it.

After extensive development work and associate training, Rice launched a price-based loyalty scheme and began identifying more than 80% of its total sales within just a few short months.

Rice Epicurean has continued to capture ever-higher levels of detailed customer information and has built a comprehensive database since its launch. The company has done an excellent job of not only committing their entire organization to a customer-focused strategy, but also redirecting past marketing expenditures to support their efforts.

Gary has assumed responsibility for leading Rice Epicurean's marketing efforts, developing a comprehensive calendar each year mapping out activities between extending both hard and soft benefits to Epicurean card members as well as focusing on recognition of their most valuable customers.

The Houston market has become a hotbed of competition with the introduction of Wal-Mart supercenters, HEB supermarkets, HEB's Central Market format, and Whole Foods. All this in addition to Kroger, Albertson's, and Safeway (through their acquisition of Randall's), along with a mixture of other independents and smaller operators has made the market very competitive. Further complicating matters, Safeway and Kroger each has a retail loyalty program and at times execute various marketing programs designed to impact customer shopping behavior.

As new competitors entered the market, it was inevitable that they would begin to directly compete with Rice Epicurean; indeed the company became aware that Whole Foods planned a new store almost directly across the street from one of Rice's oldest stores. The Whole Foods format is an upscale offering with a strong focus on natural and organic products, high quality perishables, unusual specialty products, and prepared foods: a strong competitor for Rice's target customer.

As mentioned, the Whole Foods store was opening very near one of Rice's oldest stores and the management team did a great deal of analysis on the costs of remodeling the store versus the expected return on investment. The decision was made not to make a major investment in the location and instead to close the store. What made this decision more palatable for Rice was the fact that they had two other stores within approximately one mile on either side of the threatened location, and felt confident they could move a good deal of their sales from the closing store to their two other locations, particularly in that they had a great deal of customer data gathered through their Experience Card platform.

Prior to publicly announcing the closure of the threatened store, Rice contacted each of their best customers of the store to inform them of the closing and thanking them for their past relationship. Further, the letter went on to explain the proximity of the other Rice locations and explained that the company hoped that the customers would continue shopping with them using one of the other nearby stores. To enhance this appeal, the letter included a gift thanking the customer for their past relationship and also provided inducements in the way of savings certificates to be used each week for the next six week period.

As a follow up a short time later, another letter was sent to these valuable customers who were at risk from the store managers of the two Rice Epicurean stores hoping to pick up the business. Again the correspondence thanked the customers for their past shopping and included special offers for visiting the nearby Rice Epicurean stores.

The Whole Foods store opened as scheduled and has apparently been successful; but, the success has not been realized entirely at Rice Epicurean Markets' expense. Rice Epicurean, through their use of customer information, blunted the competitive threat and was able to move over 60% of the closed store's business to their other two nearby stores; in addition raising overall profits by moving this additional business to already profitable stores without the overhead of the closed store.

I asked Gary what he would have expected of the new competitive opening if he had not had customer data. His response was that Rice Epicurean would have been lucky to retain even 10% of the closed store's business at other locations, and at a much greater cost. This story is a powerful testament to the power of strategic operations, a strong brand identity in the marketplace, and an understanding and use of customer data.

This story is also valuable in that it points out that even the most customer literate companies cannot ignore the fundamentals of retailing. Advanced use of customer information can be quite powerful, but it alone will not overcome newer, fresher competitors. Around the world we have seen that customer literacy has made good operators even better, providing them yet another way to connect with their customers.

Green Hills

Retailers can now work to align their business strategies with their operations, supported by customer-based metrics. Many CEO's and top management people do not yet appreciate the implications of this movement. Too many retailers continue to view loyalty marketing as just another marketing promotion; they do not yet realize that there is a far greater, more far-reaching strategy at work.

Green Hills is an independent supermarket located in Syracuse, NY. The same market forces described earlier are at work in the Syracuse marketplace; on any given Sunday consumers open their newspaper to find at least six full color, multi-page supermarket flyers, in addition to Wal-Mart, K-Mart, and other discounters and club stores'. The food retailing scene in the market is one of the most brutal in the U.S. While Green Hills had been able to compete and maintain its business, in no small part due to its use of customer information, it was becoming increasingly difficult.

Through a careful analysis of the market and competitors, Green Hills believed there was an opportunity to move up-market, providing larger selections of specialty, gourmet, and international foods, in addition to high quality perishable offerings. A review of its customer information reinforced this finding; the more valuable customers were already purchasing from amongst the existing limited offerings of specialty products, but it was also found that other potentially valuable customers were going elsewhere in search of products that Green Hills did not carry.

Green Hills began a concerted effort to re-brand itself, moving up-market and lessening its dependence upon traditional price promotion of national branded products. This effort was complete, encompassing the resetting of many categories, bringing a wide assortment of new specialty and natural/organic products into the store, upgrading the quality of perishable offerings, physical and décor improvements, and a concentration on training and educating store staff. Most noticeable was the change in the weekly flyer; Green Hills has transformed its flyer into a communication vehicle, educating its customers as to the high quality fresh foods and specialty products now in the store and ideas for their use. Most notable, Green Hills has not had a national brand product on the front page of the flyer for over a year's time, and yet has been able to maintain and even grow sales volume.

There were certainly many components to the repositioning of Green Hills, including renovations and décor upgrades to the physical store, remerchandising of certain product categories to make way for new sections and expanded offerings of specialty products, education and involvement of the management team and staff, and mass advertising designed to promote the Green Hills "brand" and quality foods. The ability to measure customer shopping behavior during this ongoing evolution has provided a critical comfort level to the success of these ongoing efforts.

Such a transformation can be a terrifying experience, moving from decades of traditional product-based price promotion to reliance on quality products, not sold by low price points. Having a rich knowledge of its customers and their behavior has enabled this transformation to progress at a fast pace.

Green Hills management was able to track the shopping behavior of existing customers, expecting some (the more deal-driven customers) to begin decreasing their spending and others (those who would find the changes appealing) to increase their shopping. In addition to indeed seeing these things occur the team was able to monitor the number and shopping behavior of new customers coming into the store and weigh this against the loss of the more deal-driven consumers. Tracking the total number of customer households shopping each week and comparing it to the same periods the year prior, in conjunction with monitoring the customer retention rate for both the whole store and individual departments, clearly showed what was happening during this transition.

Green Hills is located in one of the older areas of the city of Syracuse, one comprised of older middle-class neighborhoods. While maintaining and bringing along many of its existing customers was central to this change in market position, management also realized that to be successful Green Hills would have to become a destination store, drawing customers from throughout the Central New York area.

In addition to tracking new customers joining the store, Lisa Piron, Director of Information Systems for Green Hills, also monitored customer shopping by postal code, this type of information vital in gauging the success of drawing customers from further away as Green Hills moved to the destination store image versus that of a traditional supermarket. Customer activity, such as frequency of shopping and spending, were monitored by department in addition to postal codes, giving Green Hills a firm hand on what was occurring.

While maintaining its historical focus on Tier 1 and Tier 2 customers, the store also realized that it was important to begin cultivating customers interested in the higher quality and gourmet foods that were becoming the focus of the store. By analyzing the detailed shopping patterns of known "foodie" customers, Piron was able to create lifestyle-based customer segmentations that allowed her to identify potential "foodie" customers so as to include them in customer specific marketing efforts.

During the transition to a more up-market store offering very high quality fresh foods and other specialty offerings, management of Green Hills held a series of meetings with their key associates from throughout the store to explain the changes and the reasons behind them. Much of the discussion focused upon the notion of building the Green Hills brand through the customer's shopping experience. A list of all the factors impacting upon that shopping experience was developed and divided into two; those factors related to the in-store shopping experience, and those factors related to the at-home Green Hills experience.

One of the at-home factors was enjoyment of the products. Green Hills could do a terrific job of building the image of their aged Black Angus beef as the best available, creating an ambiance in the store such that a customer purchases a $50 roast to enjoy for a special meal. Anything gained in that transaction would be lost if the customer takes the roast home and does not know how to properly prepare it. If the roast comes out either raw or like shoe leather, it will not be the customer's fault; it's the terrible meat from the store. Retailers like Green Hills now have to think outside of the store; how the store can educate and assist the consumer in the preparation of the food that is purchased so that it creates an enjoyable experience at home – providing reason for a return visit. Retail is no longer confined to putting items on the shelf with price tags.

As was mentioned earlier, a key part of Green Hills' transition is in developing the store as a destination, drawing customers from a good distance to the products and experience offered. Realizing the importance of retaining new customers visiting the store for the first time, Green Hills revisited their new customer process with regard to their loyalty platform. Whereas before new customers were provided information about Green Hills and given savings offers to encourage shopping and a repeat visit, management realized that this new customer touch-point created an opportunity to make an even stronger impression on first time visitors. Customers shopping at the store for the first time and joining the loyalty program are still given information about the store – hours, forms of payment accepted, contact information for key staff members, and so on – but they are also given a gift bag containing a package of signature biscotti, made from scratch in the store's bakery. Green Hills is aware that every customer interaction provides an opportunity to build the Green Hills brand.

Green Hills could create more synergy between its product strategy and customer strategy by cross-indexing new customers with those purchasing in a gourmet food group. This process would further target those new customers that the store could more intensively nurture, reinforcing its strategies.

Further tying together its product and customer strategies, Green Hills revamped its web site, including an online shopping service for customers throughout the Central New York area. Customers could now go on-line through greenhills.com and shop for their food needs. Everything the store carried was included, from mainline products to the specialty and fresh food offerings. Lacking the high concentration of population density found in larger metropolitan areas, Green Hills chose to not offer home delivery, instead allowing customers to shop online and providing pick-up at the store; the customer only has to call from their cell phone when approaching the store, an associate meeting them in the parking lot with their order.

The Green Hills story brings to light an important fact: even the best retail customer-focused marketing effort is not enough when confronted by profound change within a channel. As Wal-Mart opens up more and more supercenters, they are cutting a wide swath through the traditional supermarket industry. Knowing that Green Hills could not compete on a commodity battleground, Green Hills has developed a new product strategy: repositioning the store in the marketplace and using its customer knowledge to assist in that repositioning.

The Kroger Company and Wal-Mart: Battle of the giants...

The market forces of consolidation, commoditization, and channel blurring also constrain the profitability and growth of even larger companies.

As discussed in Chapter One, Wal-Mart is having a profound impact on food retailing in the U.S. market. Dr. Ira Kalish of Retail Forward predicts in his report "The Age of Wal-Mart" that within the next few years Wal-Mart will operate over 2,000 Supercenters and that food sales at Wal-Mart will account for approximately one-third of the national increase in spending on food. [1]

Wal-Mart's growth in the supermarket channel is causing even the largest companies to re-think their strategy moving forward. Attempting to address the Wal-Mart colossus head-on with a price-based strategy is sure to be unsuccessful. One needs to look no further than Kmart for proof.

It has been reported that Wal-Mart's operating overhead (sales, general, and administrative costs) is in the realm of 15.5%. Grocery stores' operating overhead averages 24% according to the Food Marketing Institute. [2] Such a gap is causing even the largest supermarket companies to reevaluate their strategy. No matter the amount of cost cutting, the average supermarket company will be unable to approach Wal-Mart's low overhead, leaving supermarkets at a severe disadvantage. Not surprisingly, we have recently seen the larger supermarket companies, such as Kroger, Albertsons, and Safeway, tout that their strategic advantage in the coming battles is "convenience"; their companies offering smaller, easier-to-shop stores, neighborhood locations and easier access. Perhaps some readers remember when the local independent supermarkets touted convenience as one of their prime advantages when the larger chain stores began entering their markets. It may be that convenience is not the strategic strength that some think.

The impact of Wal-Mart on food retailing is considerable. For example, as Wal-Mart opened supercenter stores in Albertson's (the second largest U.S. traditional supermarket company) home market of Boise, Idaho, Albertsons' market share plummeted from 65% to 37%. [3] While stating that it will not enter into a price war with Wal-Mart, Albertsons will be hard pressed to maintain its sales volume and core business by trying to compete on other factors.

Kroger, the United States' largest traditional food retailer, has publicly announced that their corporate strategy in the years to come, as the battle with Wal-Mart intensifies, will be that of an aggregator, rolling up smaller supermarket companies that can no longer compete. Joseph Pichler, CEO of Kroger said the strategy "plays to our economic advantage. Fifty percent of the market share in our major markets is held by competitors who do not have economies of scale, who are not supercenters and who are not even strong regional operators." [4] Kroger will maintain sales growth by acquiring smaller regional supermarket companies that can no longer compete.

While this strategy may make some sense, it does not address another weapon in Wal-Mart's arsenal, that of their more conventional supermarket offering: Neighborhood Markets. Neighborhood Markets are typically about 40,000 square feet in size and feature conventional food offerings in addition to an in-store pharmacy. In areas where these stores are already operating, studies have shown that their prices are on average 30% less than conventional supermarkets. [5] Wal-Mart has publicly announced that they will open over 550 Neighborhood Market stores across the U.S. within the next five years. [6] Their intention is to position them in between Wal-Mart supercenters, thus picking up the smaller food shopping trips consumers typically make in between visits to the supercenters.

Kroger's strategy of aggregation does not address the threat posed by Wal-Mart in the long term. Eventually Kroger must find a way to overcome the structural differences between their cost structure and Wal-Mart's, so as to support a higher price position with consumers. Being an aggregator is perhaps an acceptable strategy in the short term, but it will not ensure long term success. "That's what's deluding some of the chains," said Iowa State University economist Kenneth Stone, who has published numerous studies on Wal-Mart's impact on competitors. "Kroger is picking up market share from smaller independents going out of business. But that can only last so long. Then, they're going to have to fight Wal-Mart head-to-head and the competition will be a lot tougher." [7]

Before any readers outside food retailing relax, consider what may happen in other channels if Wal-Mart were to pursue a similar strategy. It has been reported that Wal-Mart has for some time now considered a move into the drug store channel, in which it sees great opportunity. What would be the impact if

Wal-Mart were to move into the sporting goods channel, or clothing, or electronics; any product area with which it has experience. As a $200 billion per year company, Wal-Mart will become ever more aggressive as it tries to maintain growth so as to support its share price.

It has been recently announced that the 99 Cents Only chain will create a gourmet food section in their 140 stores. Another report explains that other stores in this same sector are considering merchandising gourmet foods in their stores. In return, Wal-Mart is now experimenting with creating "everything for a dollar" sections in some stores; speculation is that they may enter this retail segment with dedicated stores. No retail channel is safe from threat. Such are the perils of competing solely on a product-based business model in a world which is rapidly becoming commoditized.

Kroger has one of the largest customer databases in the world today, capturing customer data through every division in the company save one. How can they make use of it in their battles with Wal-Mart?

One of the first areas is to use customer data to assist in making expenditures on marketing and advertising as efficient as possible. One of the larger expenditures supermarket companies have in this area are their weekly flyers, typically distributed through newspapers or some other delivery method, often done by a postal code or carrier route basis.

Many times supermarket retailers find that they can realize substantial savings related to their flyers by doing an analysis cross-indexing their best customers with the number of flyers distributed in a given postal code or area. This type analysis usually produces findings that can lead to much more efficiency in the distribution of flyers without hurting sales, at substantial cost savings to the company.

Kroger could carry this concept further, learning what categories and products most appeal to their more valuable customers within each of their marketing regions. By determining this, the company could then intensify negotiations with the manufacturers of those goods, thereby being able to feature the products more frequently or reduce the everyday shelf prices so as to help retain those more valuable customers.

Understanding that higher spending customers offer much higher profit margins than lower spending consumers, Kroger could begin skewing its marketing investments to reward customers for their shopping behavior over time, thus creating more higher spending customers within its customer base. For such a strategy to be effective however, Kroger would need discipline with the redirection of monies.

Within each division Kroger could create reporting which would measure the cost of markdown expense and allocate it across different customer tiers, thus providing a benchmarking system. By withdrawing some of this markdown, and instead redirecting those funds to support different loyalty-building initiatives (such as the Web Miles program), Kroger could begin to build the proportion of higher spending customers within its customer base, benefiting from the increased profitability resulting from such changes.

The next step would be to establish measures of customer retention, for both new customers and existing customers, within each Kroger division, such measures being produced for each individual store. After educating management as to the meaning of these measures, and ways in which customer retention can be impacted, we would foresee that Kroger tie the store management team's incentive pay to these measures. This would quickly and powerfully begin to align the manager's actions with those of long term benefit to the company; retaining more and more customers over time, in turn building sales.

Within each division, Kroger could then begin providing special offers to their best customers; products that are relevant and valued by the customer, not offers that are manufacturer driven. This is an important point; time and again retailers turn to manufacturers to fund their marketing efforts, including special offers to best customers. Manufacturers are often willing to do this, providing they have some say in which consumers receive which offer, a tactic that can be at odds with the retailer's strategy. The goal of this practice is to provide value to the consumer relative to brands and products the individual consumer prefers. Sending an offer for a discount on a competing brand is not of value to the consumer. This practice, targeted to the best customers or top customer tier, can strongly promote customer recognition which in turn increases customer retention, increasing spending and profits.

As for secondary customers, or Tier 2 customers, Kroger could then begin to do a gap analysis, determining which customers are not purchasing in specific categories. The goal here would be to deliver to the customer a mix of offers, some of preferred brands and products they do purchase, and other offers perhaps non-brand specific to foster purchasing in previously ignored categories.

While retaining their customer segmentations used for management and financial reporting, Kroger could evolve to segmentations used for marketing purposes, creating lifestyle-based segments. Marketing and promotion then begins to shift with the company now marketing a different mix of information, offers, and services to each lifestyle group. Again, the goal of such practices is to foster customer retention and purchasing, the customer data providing a measurement tool to gauge the effectiveness of these initiatives. For example, Kroger has stated that they will stress natural and organic products in their stores; this strategy lends itself handily to a lifestyle-based marketing initiative.

What is perhaps a movement in this direction is signaled by Kroger's potential relationship with Dunnhumby, a company specializing in data mining and analytics, the driver behind Tesco's Clubcard program in the U.K. By utilizing Dunnhumby's expertise, Kroger may be moving towards developing more specialized customer segmentations based upon customers' lifestyles and delivering targeted offers to them.

Will Kroger capitalize on its customer data, using it as a strategic asset in the competitive store battles, or will it fall back on the traditional mass marketing of old? Attempting to compete using only the same-price-for-all mass retailing tactics is a losing proposition when competing with Wal-Mart, as Kmart discovered. Kroger's opportunity lies in discovering those consumers preferring their stores and product lines, providing them with special pricing, recognition, and services so as to retain them over time. Will Kroger become customer intelligent? Time will tell.

Customer-based strategies growing globally...

The rise of customer intelligence in retail is happening globally; retailers on every continent are actively gathering customer data. Their challenge is in properly understanding and using the data, turning it into valuable information and knowledge.

Japan provides a fascinating large-scale view of the perils of modern retailing.

There are many parallels between the state of retailing today in Japan and that of the United States retail markets some twenty years ago. There exist a multitude of smaller retailers in many channels and the distribution system is composed of a number of layers, all contributing to an inefficient, fragmented retail industry when compared to such other markets in the world as North America or Europe.

This structure, combined with the poor economic conditions that have existed in Japan for the past several years, puts the domestic retail industry in a precarious position, very much at risk from global competitors entering the market. And it is this that is beginning to occur as companies such as Wal-Mart, Carrefour, Costco and others eye a huge market ripe for the taking.

Realizing that they are at risk from outside competitors, and looking for internal growth, Japanese retailers began to fervently study retail frequent shopper programs in the late 1990s in the U.S. market and Europe. Hoping to use such marketing programs to build sales and lower advertising costs, Japanese retailers sought a solution that would help address their challenges.

Frequent shopper programs began to explode through Japanese retailing, almost all being points-based programs; many of them operated without capturing detailed customer information. Many Japanese retailers have made the same mistake that other retailers have made the world over: thinking that a marketing program alone would cure their ills. Unfortunately, gaining customer knowledge, and making effective use of it, is not a simple matter.

There are many examples throughout Japan of retailers tiring of their frequent shopper or retail loyalty program efforts. In many cases, these points programs have simply become a new form of price discounting with certain retailers offering triple points, or even more, for purchasing specified products or shopping on certain days of the month. Without the benefit of capturing detailed customer data, such efforts are destined to lose their effectiveness as others simply offer even more points; analogous to lowering prices even further in hopes of luring consumers.

But amongst this frenzy are a select few companies that understand the long term strategy of customer intelligence. And it is these companies that offer the best hope for the success of the domestic Japanese retail industry.

Mitsubishi has understood the power of gathering, understanding, and using detailed customer information on a large scale for several years, having done a great deal of study in the North American and European markets. Their strategy for capitalizing on this area is a multi-pronged, long range vision.

The translation of computer database software systems used in the U.S. or European markets to Japanese kanji-based software is a very expensive and time consuming process. Given this condition, and a lack of proper systems and tools to support retail customer knowledge platforms, Mitsubishi realized that they must create the tools for retailers to utilize.

The formation of a subsidiary, Customer Communications, Ltd. (cust-communications.com), was the first step in this direction. Customer Communications was charged with developing the software tools and infrastructure required by retailers to capture and use customer data. While a work-in-progress, Customer Communications has been supporting retail platforms for some time now, providing the retailer with regular reporting drawn from their data in addition to providing consulting services to assist the retailer with an understanding of the information and providing direction for use.

While Customer Communications is able to support any retail channel with their customer knowledge efforts (they count both supermarkets and chain drug stores amongst their clients), the area of food retailing is one of particular interest to Mitsubishi. The Consumer Products division of Mitsubishi is one of Japan's largest importers of food products as well as being a large producer in its own right. This combination provides Mitsubishi with the potential for streamlining the promotion of such products by linking customer purchase behavior, gleaned through the retailer's customer data, with the marketing and promotion of specific brands and products. Furthermore, by having strong relationships with a number of food wholesalers and distributors throughout the country, Mitsubishi, through its Customer Communications subsidiary, is well positioned to make use of customer intelligence on a number of levels.

Mitsubishi is pursuing a far ranging strategy based upon customer intelligence. Providing technologies and systems is only a small part of their game plan. Yasuo Yamamoto, General Manager of Marketing Business Development in the Consumer Business Division, is expanding his company's reach and knowledge through the formation of strategic alliances on the web and across other customer touch-points, understanding that customer data, properly understood and utilized, presents strong strategic opportunities.

It is through efforts such as these that the Japanese domestic retailing industry hopes to blunt the attack of outside global competitors. Certainly these efforts alone will not win the day, but when paired with adopting other best practices, such as streamlining the distribution system and developing other efficiencies, the strategy of customer intelligence is a very powerful one.

RETAIL-TO-ONE:
THE LEADING EDGE

During a recent threshold program, M&M Meat Shops determined that it was time to move forward with customer communications. Linking the MAX database with their website, M&M Meat Shops allowed customers to check spending progress toward earning their reward, providing a summary of transactions to date during the program. Further, the customer could learn which MAX card numbers are linked together in the database to create the customer's household information. Customers finding mistakes e-mail the office where corrective action is taken. This is another factor in maintaining the accuracy of customer data over time, actively involving the customer in the process.

Going a step further, M&M Meat Shops conducted a trial of kiosks in several stores for the same purpose of communicating customer specific information. A customer entering the store could swipe their MAX card at the kiosk and learn of their spending to date on the current reward program. Providing such information to customers, especially while they are in the store shopping, can be very powerful.

The capability put in place by M&M Meat Shops through its website and kiosks in the store is creating the foundation for communication of yet more customer specific information. Once the base capability is in place, providing a customer with the ability to access their specific information, it is an easy step to providing customer specific offers and information, all designed to encourage increased shopping and customer retention.

M&M Meat Shops is one of a handful of retail companies about the world putting the communication tools in place allowing them to progress in the evolution towards a one-to-one retail environment. We are seeing an increasing number of companies pursuing more efficient communications with their customers, utilizing messaging on the POS tickets provided the consumer at checkout, or through the retailer's website. A few pioneers, such as Rice Epicurean Markets, are increasingly relying on e-mail to communicate with their valued clientele.

Rather than mailing a paper copy of their weekly flyer to regular customers who reside outside the flyer's distribution area, Rice Epicurean has begun e-mailing the weekly flyer to these people, with negligible downside. In the past, Rice Epicurean has relied on special newspaper advertisements and direct mail to interested customers to promote the company's special one day meat sales, which occur several times each year. Rice is increasingly finding that using e-mail to communicate with customers is providing a better return on their marketing and communication costs related to the meat sale than paper-based communications.

Keihoku, a small food retailer with several stores in the greater Tokyo area, mails its Gold and Silver customers a small catalog each month listing the various items the customer can purchase during the month at special pricing; the pricing differentiated by customer segment. The prices are delivered electronically at the point of sale by the customer using their loyalty card.

Other Japanese retailers are even more advanced. Nissho, a 27 store supermarket chain, promotes a service they call "e-mail flyer". Consumers can access the flyer through their computers or via their mobile phones; over 6 million Japanese consumers are online through their internet-enabled mobile phone. Customers participating in the "e-mail flyer" program receive daily updates on product promotions and special prices, in addition to other information. [1]

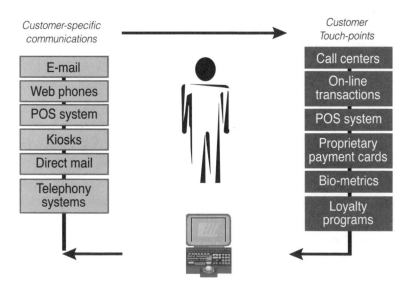

Green Hills has long had the capability to deliver differentiated pricing to customers through its POS, and has made good use of it. Rather than go to market having to extend low price points on popular items to everyone, Green Hills extends special pricing to its top customer tiers, informing customers by way of direct mail; the customer receives the price electronically at the POS, triggered by their loyalty card.

Tesco has recently announced that it will begin distributing product-specific coupons, targeted using data from its Clubcard database, at the checkout. [2] *While these coupons will automatically be printed by the POS at checkout, can the day be far off when Tesco will make such offers available to their individual customers over the internet, or through kiosks in the stores, intercepting customers prior to checkout?*

In Japan, millions of consumers are online each day through their mobile phones. Each phone contains a GPS chip, allowing the service provider to track where any phone is at any point in time. Some retailers are availing themselves of a service which allows them to send targeted e-mails to consumers within a certain distance of their shops.

Around the world, retailers have begun putting in place the bits and picccs needed to electronically communicate and deliver offers and information to support a retailing-to-one strategy. What has been missing is one retailer, or systems vendor, putting in place all the necessary systems and tools to bring such an environment to fruition in a mass retail setting.

But this situation is about to change.

The retail industry is at the dawn of a new age; a revolution coming in the way retail companies are structured and organized; in the economic model used in going to market; and in communications to the consumer. This retail revolution is being driven by the fusion of previously disparate systems into a cohesive whole, enabling processes that heretofore were simply not feasible.

To better appreciate these new capabilities, it is perhaps best to begin with an explanation of the obstacles that have hindered further development and use of customer data in the retail industry. Some of these obstacles have been created by limits in technology, but others lie within the inertia resulting from decades of product-based business.

Many large retailers were early adopters of database technology, having to track information related to an enormous number of products. The trends of consolidation and channel blurring have served only to further increase the amount of product-based information that must be stored and analyzed, as retailers must bring into their systems local products from companies they have absorbed, and products from outside their traditional channel. Amongst larger retail companies there is a patchwork of legacy information systems, cobbled together as companies have grown and new technologies have come to the fore.

A prevalent practice growing from conventional database wisdom has been the building of data silos, a system of storing like information within one data structure so as to increase the speed of analysis and access. For the past several decades, companies have built data silos containing vendor and product-based data; product movement, sales information, cost data, and so on.

When the first frequent shopper programs began appearing in retail, the companies operating such programs created yet another separate data structure for their customer data, many times using solutions which housed customer data within their own systems, sometimes in proprietary formats. Many times these loyalty database solutions also included some level of product data, but not to the extent of the retailer's primary systems.

This in turn created a situation whereby retail companies now have important data residing in two or more disparate systems; product-based data stored in one (or more) data silo, and customer-based data (customer sales, visits, etc.) stored in a separate data silo. This structure has created the proverbial brick wall, making it very difficult for retailers to fully integrate their product and customer data.

Imagine for a moment that you are a traditional product category manager. Historically, your view of the world has been limited to product-based data, ideally, scan-based product movement data gleaned from the POS system. Additionally, this movement data has been married with some level of product cost information facilitating at least an estimate of category profitability.

Given that your responsibility is to grow both sales and profits of your category, how do you go about it?

Product-Based Merchandising

- Active purchasers
  - *Heavy buyers*
  - *Ocasional buyers*
  - *Infrequent buyers*
- Non-purchasers
- Brand loyal
- Switchers
- Trade monies

Most likely you would begin with an analysis of your category; looking at sales, unit movement, and share of market. You would probably measure the markdown expense and average selling price per item. Perhaps you would measure your category sales and gross profit per linear foot of selling space, so as to ascertain the category productivity. With this information serving as a benchmark, you set off to drive business.

What tools do you have at your disposal? Certainly point of purchase signs and inclusion of category products in the company's mass marketing vehicles (ad flyers, radio and television spots, etc.) are possibilities. Your most potent weapon is probably the mainstay of traditional retailing: temporary advertised specials or price discounts to drive sales volume. While such promotions can indeed drive additional sales, there is an added cost in the related markdown expense. And many retail companies find that it takes increasing amounts of markdown to drive equivalent net sales.

If you are creative you may partner with vendors so as to tap into their consumer databases or purchase direct mail lists from third parties. Such direct mail efforts are expensive – while vendors may agree to support them, they will want to structure the effort to their advantage. And certainly, you negotiate with vendors for trade monies, offering them ad placement, shelf placement, and any other benefit you can think of in return.

If you are truly ambitious, you may undertake a study of your supply chain logistics, looking for any possible savings that can translate to increased margin or lower retail prices (which hopefully will help drive turnover). For the technology-inclined category manager, there is dynamic pricing; analysis of item movement across the entire category so as to identify the maximum yield from each item (the point of maximum revenue identified by analyzing movement at different price levels).

This has been the world of product merchandisers; all measures relating to the product; the view of the world stopping at the shelf edge; knowing there are customers purchasing but not being able to "see" them.

But now let's shift our view to the polar opposite of product myopicism and view our stores through the eyes of a customer category manager; an entirely different perspective. Whereas the product category manager's view stopped at the shelf edge, the customer category manager's view ends at the shopping cart, able to see the items purchased but unable to view the category and department organizational system. This is essentially the limited view offered by customer data based in its own silo.

Imagine now that you are a "customer category" manager charged with growing the sales and margins from your category, in addition to improving retention of your assets over time (controlling shrink). How do you proceed?

Customer-Based Merchandising

Drawing on your knowledge of Best Customer marketing, you design various incentives and enticements to encourage customers to increase their spending, not caring what specific products or services they may purchase.

- Customer Value
- Customer Preferred...
  - Categories
  - Brands
  - Sizes
- Related Products
- Shopping Motivation:
  - Relationship
  - Deal Driven

You may even go so far as to begin redirecting your markdown expense and other marketing-related expenditures, allocating them across customer segments seeking to bring income streams and value received into alignment. Properly done, you are able to increase the proportion of higher spending customers within the company's customer base, thus improving profitability. You are able to accomplish your goals, meanwhile oblivious to the specific product purchases being made by your customers.

Just as the product category manager can grow sales without giving thought to who is purchasing the product, the customer category manager can grow purchases without thought or care given to particular brands or items.

Vastly simplifying the process, the customer manager can readily grow sales, not only by enticing with incentives, but by providing deals on products and categories known to interest the individual customer. While this may maximize customer performance, it may wreak havoc with product category performance. I am presenting such extremely opposite views of merchandising for a purpose; so that the reader can appreciate the power unleashed by integrating a product-based and customer-based view of merchandising.

This obstacle precludes retail companies from fully exploring the world of their sales floors, understanding the interplay between customers and products; at different times, at different prices, and different merchandising displays. Many times even more basic information is unobtainable, such as viewing a complete product category over a period of time, measuring movement and sales in total and by customer tier or by heavy category purchasers or light brand buyers.

Companies can, and do, carry out tremendous amounts of analysis attempting to learn all they can relative to customer shopping behavior and specific categories or products. But such studies tend to be one-off efforts, special reports to address specific questions or opportunities; these efforts are not robust enough to provide for an everyday operating system allowing a retailer to fully intertwine the disparate data together in a meaningful way.

Furthermore, if a retailer can access the desired data, they are constrained in their ability to execute on it. It is one thing to learn of customer behavior relative to product purchasing, but if no action can be taken, what good is it? And if the retailer can drill down and isolate a segment of customers he wishes to provide an offer to, in most cases he is limited to having to use a paper-based offer or coupon, delivered via direct mail. In today's world, the time and expense involved in devising a mail program, generating the offers and targeted customer lists, printing the communications, delivering the piece through the postal system, and then waiting for customer response so as to evaluate the success or failure of the campaign is far too long and far too expensive. Time is as much a competitive weapon today as cost control.

Beyond communicating offers on a customer specific basis is the actual delivery of the offer at checkout. A majority of retail companies possessing some level of customer data are still confined to using a paper-based coupon to deliver a specific offer to a customer at the POS. Yes, it is possible to e-mail coupon offers, but they still must be printed out and presented by the customer at checkout.

To bring these obstacles into a real-world focus, think in terms of the following process. Traditionally, a product category manager or buyer will meet with the vendor to discuss marketing plans and product purchasing. In a good situation, the buyer is able to access some level of product movement data; ideally, data accurate relative to the entire category and the vendor's brands in particular. If the buyer wished to view the brand's movement relative to customer tiers, chances are it would call for a special report produced by the customer loyalty group over in the marketing department or even a special effort by the IT department.

There are retail companies that have cobbled together their information systems in order to produce reporting for their buyers and category managers showing the movement of products within a category by different customer segments; typically the customer segments are based upon spending and are shown as two to three groups, such as the top 30% of customers, middle 40%, and bottom 30%. So now the buyer is able to show the vendor who of their customers is purchasing specific brands. Possibly good information, but to what affect? Even if the buyer were able to access information at a more detailed level, there are severe limits as to actions that can be taken.

Some retail companies work with vendors in assembling targeted promotions, based upon customer purchasing behavior, the offers funded by the vendors. But even these efforts involve a tremendous amount of work and coordination between the buyers, the marketing department, and the information systems group. And, with rare exception, these types of initiatives continue to be paper-based, requiring the customer to present a paper coupon at checkout to receive the special offer. Such efforts to target offers and promotions to individual customers, or even customer groups, involve too much time, coordination, and expense; the flywheel of a one-price-for-all philosophy having too much momentum to be slowed by the friction involved in data analysis, offer creation, communication, and delivery issues to change course towards more customer specific retailing.

So what is technology bringing to the table that will so strongly influence on this situation? There are two pieces to the technology puzzle that, when fused together, create an infrastructure facilitating retail companies going to market on an individual customer basis.

The first technological advance addresses the brick wall that has formed due to multiple data structures hobbling access to the entirety of product and customer data. What heretofore have been separate systems are now combined into one data structure, a platform, allowing the retailer to easily analyze and access any view of their data; from viewing product movement by customer segments to viewing a customer segment's purchasing behavior across all products. Utilizing new software technologies, all a retail company's data can now reside in one data structure, accessible by anyone via a web browser (having security clearance). This opens up a retailer's information vault to users across the company, not just those located at head office with access to the data systems.

No longer is there one proprietary system for maintaining vendor information and another for product movement drawn from the POS systems, and yet another for maintenance of customer data. All the functionality needed by a retail company is fully integrated across a common platform, each function drawing from and writing to a common data structure, containing all product and customer-related data.

To continue with our previous example, with a platform approach, the buyer can quickly and easily access not only the vendor's product movement, but can also begin to slice and dice the movement relative to different customer segments, all while sitting at his desk with the vendor. Further, the buyer and vendor together can discuss and project costs and potential returns for targeting specific product offers to specific customer segments, again, all taking place almost instantaneously using cube software technology.

Merging this information, companies are now able to see the customers behind the product sales; additionally, having knowledge of those customers who are non-purchasers. Analysts can now segment category customers into groups such as heavy buyers, occasional purchasers, or light users. Further, we can combine this perspective with brand level and item level movement data.

You now have a new world of information available to you, expanding your view of the category and customer activity. Your responsibilities as a merchandiser remain the same: maximize sales and profits. How do you proceed?

Holistic View of Merchandising Provided by Integrating Customer and Product Views

Customer View

Product View

First we must revisit the reporting and benchmarks used for performance measurement. In addition to the product data / customer tier matrix, we must create measurements for tracking our markdown expense (akin to mass advertising) and our customer-focused marketing expenditures so that we can seek the proper balance between the two over time.

You might begin by segmenting customers into those purchasing in the category and those not, perhaps experimenting with offers to the non-purchasers in efforts to draw them into the category. Next, you can segment the active category customers into groups, such as heavy buyers, medium users, and light purchasers, developing different offers for each. Becoming more advanced, you overlay the customer lifecycle concept, apply-ing it to a category; marketing to new customers of the category, seeking to increase purchasing and retention of those regularly buying, and working to retain those customers declining in category activity.

As you gain knowledge of how your category customers and products interact over time, you begin to see the correlations between customers and specific brands; those customers that are deal-seekers versus the regular buyers.

Once our buyer has identified a target customer segment and built appropriate offers, he can then send the information to be communicated to the customer via electronic-based communication vehicles: kiosks in the store, via e-mail to the customer, by the customer logging into the retailer's website, through telephone-based systems, and even through the POS systems in the stores. Companies such as Tribeworks, headquartered in San Francisco, specialize in the creation of communication vehicles such as kiosks or web sites to com-municate the content created by the retailer's customer intelligence system.

There has been no miraculous, overnight advance in technology to accomplish this. Rather, it has been the slow, methodical evolution leading to what are now robust systems designed to work in the dynamic environment of a mass retail company. The continual growth of the consumer population using the internet to source information, and the ever-growing use of e-mail as a pre-ferred communication vehicle, are contributing to the feasibility of this model.

But we're not done yet. In addition to the customer specific offers being com-municated to the customer using the aforementioned vehicles, the offers are also sent to the company's POS systems, accessible to each individual store's POS system across the retailer's chain. When the customer identifies herself at checkout by use of her loyalty card, fingerprint scan, or proprietary payment card, the system automatically delivers the offers the customer is entitled to. The POS system itself is an integral part of the information systems platform.

In a sense, such a system finally closes the loop, allowing the creation of customer specific offers drawn from the analysis of customer purchasing behavior, the communication of those offers to the individual customer on a cost effective basis, and the actual delivery of the offer electronically at the point of sale. What is being created by these advances is a frictionless marketing environment to support retailing to the individual customer.

If this all sounds like science fiction, consider this: a system such as the one described here will be available soon after this book is published. The capabilities offered by systems like this will have a profound effect on how retailers go to market. Retalix (retalix.com), one of the largest retail software companies, is bringing such a product to market, leveraging their StoreLine POS software system (used by companies such as Tesco and the Welcome Break Group in the U.K. and Albertson's in the U.S.), and combining it with a full suite of back office systems, price book management, and customer analysis tools. The company's ReMA platform (Retalix e-Market Application) is a sophisticated web-based platform that allows retailers to easily access numerous applications to perform a wide range of business functions and provides for an unprecedented level of integration. [3]

This is not some untested, vapor-ware system that sounds incredible but has never seen the sales floor, but the merger of existing, proven technologies and systems into a coherent whole, providing for the birth of a truly holistic retail environment. A retail company now having readily available any and all information on both products sold and customers shopped; the ability to sensibly create and deliver customer-relevant promotions and offers designed to maximize customer lifetime value.

While not as advanced as the ReMA platform, other retail companies are headed in similar directions. Sears has combined two data systems into one 70 terabyte enterprise wide platform providing for a single view of their business across channels and segments. "This was driven by the needs of the business to do more analysis and more targeting of our customers," said Ben Bernstein of Sears. "What we've done is combine the customer warehouse with the ledger and inventory system on a single platform." [4]

Hudson Bay Company, Canada's largest retail company, has also brought into one data structure all the customer information relating to its nearly 10 million loyalty program participants. "We see the behavior for the customer no matter where they shop", says Rob Shields, VP, CRM, referring to the company's several banners[5]. Prior to its latest CRM strategy, each of the four store groups operated systems independent of each other, creating barriers to a comprehensive view of its customers.

The development and implementation of this functionality has profound implications for the retail industry as a whole. To fully appreciate the implications of this paradigm-shifting capability we must step back and take a much broader view of the retail industry, both from an economic and organizational perspective.

Inevitably, retail companies will view such functionality as furthering the sale of products on a more efficient basis. Some, I am sure, will search for new ways to leverage this capability by attempting to tap even more trade monies from manufacturers, able now to efficiently target and deliver specific offers which can be used in support of various brand-building initiatives.

As we discussed early on in Chapter 1, the retail industry has been heavily influenced by trade monies, financial incentives provided by manufacturers to prompt retailers to feature the manufacturer's brands in advertisements, allotted shelf space, and store displays. These monies have, in many cases, become a revenue center for retail companies, a necessary line item on the retailer's income statement contributing to profitability. Such monies are understandable in terms of traditional retail advertising, but what is their role in the coming retail world of one-to-one rather than one-to-many?

In a mass marketing, one-to-many environment, retailers could, to a degree, blind themselves to the impact of promoting certain items to raise trade monies, rather than studying the impact of such items on customer behavior Retailers bereft of customer intelligence possess no way of knowing whether the promotion of a certain product serves to attract valuable customers or deal-seekers; at the end of the day the retail company has raised more trade monies to go into their coffers, so what does it matter? Certainly, the retailer must continue to generate traffic and sales through their stores, but the point is that many times companies are product-driven, giving less heed to customer desires in the retailer's merchandising initiatives.

As we have learned through the course of our study, a product manufacturer's agenda can be quite different from a retailer's; the manufacturer interested in moving cases, regardless of the retail store it goes through, the retailer not so much caring what specific brands are sold, so long as customers buy from the retailer's stores. Will the practices fostered by trade monies now manifest themselves within this new capability which allows retailers to go to market on an individual customer basis, or will other practices develop?

In a 1997 study, Anderson Consulting found the cost of trade promotion in the grocery industry to be in excess of $30 billion. What is of even more importance, exit interviews conducted during the course of the study found that significant numbers of consumers would have purchased the promoted items at full price. [6] The practice of deal pricing, the manufacturer extending a special cost for a temporary period of time to foster sales, has been a by-product of the predominant one-price-for-all retail marketing philosophy. While trade monies are prevalent in the food retailing sector, in total, consumer-goods companies spend over $100 billion each year in trade monies and promotions. [7]

Many retailers, of all sizes, negotiate with vendors for trade monies, said monies being directed to help subsidize certain expenses incurred by the retailer. For example, retailers taking ad placement fees and using them to subsidize the cost of their advertising are sometimes obscuring the true cost of their advertising and effectively increasing their cost of goods. Manufacturers have a certain pool of monies available for retail accounts, how the retailer wants the money open to negotiation. Companies such as Wal-Mart are much more disciplined, directing vendors to credit all such trade monies to lowering the everyday cost of the product, in turn providing the retailer with a true and stable cost of goods, day in and day out. It may make sense at this point for other retailers to develop a similar discipline in purchasing product at an everyday-low-cost basis. The procurement function must be revisited by management.

By disciplining themselves to put all vendor subsidies into lowering the cost of product, retailers can now increase their gross profit margin over the course of time, granting the customer specific retailer the ability to direct discounts to the appropriate customers in order to maximize customer purchasing and value. In this way the customer specific retailer is able to invest a portion of his gross margin for the best return on investment. In practice this may mean extending a more significant price reduction to deal driven shoppers on certain items while directing a more shallow price reduction to the most valuable customers, further subsidizing the relationship with soft benefits more appreciated by this segment in lieu of deeper discounts.

In a number of retail sectors a case can be made that a good portion of the marketing message emanating from retailers has, in actuality, originated from the manufacturers and vendors; this message in the form of promotional monies and allowances tied to specific products. Essentially, manufacturers have pushed chosen products through the supply chain through the use of promotional monies, or have attempted to pull products through by issuing coupons to end consumers, relying upon the consumers to request retail stores carry the products. Retail companies seizing control of the customer relationship must now assume responsibility for marketing and advertising, the retailer knowing the preferences of their individual customers and having to combine this with the company's strategy related to product offerings.

The paradigm-shifting capabilities presented by the fusion of platform data systems and customer specific communication vehicles may also impact heavily on the organizational structure of retail companies.

To a large degree, category managers and buyers have dictated the advertising and merchandising messages delivered to consumers. The products and prices in the weekly flyer or periodic catalog are placed there by the buyers, who in turn have most likely received some type of subsidy from the vendor. In the environment described above, does this product-driven way of going to market offer a retail company the best return on investment?

Some companies will continue to go to market with a product-led focus, albeit with much more capability than possessed before. For example, the buyer can now work with the vendor to design promotions targeted at desired customer segments, estimate the cost and potential return, and send the offer off to be communicated and delivered to the customer.

But I believe other retailers will begin to appreciate the value of shifting their focus to the customer, looking to leverage this capability by providing a more meaningful shopping experience to the consumer. Rather than producing one ad flyer for thousands of customers, the retailer can essentially create an ad flyer for each individual customer containing the products and information that are meaningful to the individual. This sets the stage for a different organizational structure necessary for maximizing this capability.

A typical retail company is organized along product-defined areas, each category or department having a manager or executive responsible for it, many times the executive's incentive-based financial remuneration linked to the sales and profit performance of his or her operational area. As we learned earlier, customer intelligent retail companies segment customers to reflect the different financial values offered via customer tier reporting. Does it not make sense, then, that such Customer Tiers have their own responsible executive, a Customer Portfolio manager?

The term Customer Portfolio manager is suggested for the reason that within each customer tier, there exist subsidiary customer segments derived from marketing perspectives such as lifestyle attributes, demographics, and so on. The result is a customer portfolio, containing customers of similar economic value, sub-divided into lifestyle or demographic groupings for marketing purposes. For example, in a supermarket setting, a Customer Portfolio containing Tier One (most valuable) customers may include sub-segments of customers grouped by lifestyle, such as gourmet, natural and organic, pet, and so on.

Retail companies (with rare exception) are profit-driven institutions. It follows then, that, for organizational purposes, customer tiers based on financial value to the enterprise lead, marketing derived segmentations following. The responsibility of the Customer Portfolio manager is that of maximizing the value of his or her portfolio through increasing customer purchasing and increasing customer retention, the portfolio manager's financial incentives linked to such measures.

A close approximation for this position may be a brand manager in a consumer packaged goods company. Brand managers have complete responsibility for a brand, from production levels to marketing, the financial performance of the brand determining the brand manager's success or failure. Likewise, a customer portfolio manager becomes responsible for the sales and retention of the customers in her portfolio, able to access company resources to assist in merchandising and providing lifestyle information in communications to the customer. These resources may take the form of a product library sorted by category and/or available deals in addition to marketing groups providing lifestyle-specific information relative to the marketing-driven customer segments used by the company.

Perhaps it would be easiest to work through an actual example of how such a process would function. Let's go back to the Carol Customer and her department store example used earlier. Carol is a Tier 1 customer of the store, due to the fact she does most of her channel purchasing there. The Tier 1 Customer Portfolio manager, responsible for retaining Carol's business, draws from the various deals and lifestyle information assembled by the procurement and marketing departments to assemble relevant offers and information to be directed to Carol.

The traditional hierarchy found in retail organizations may no longer be the most effective model for this new retail enterprise; it maintains too strong a product focus to allow it to maximize customer performance. This is one of the reasons that many retail companies have been stymied in their use of customer data thus far; the typical retail organization optimized for a product-based view of the world in which a product culture permeates every facet of the organization from job positions and responsibilities to financial incentives.

It may be that a new retail organizational structure will emerge, one that is more horizontal in appearance, acknowledging the new flow of information and value through the company to the individual consumer. In this type of model, procurement and marketing functions serve a supportive role to the Customer Portfolio manager, who has ultimate responsibility for coordinating offers and information to the consumer, and whose performance is assessed relative to customer behavior.

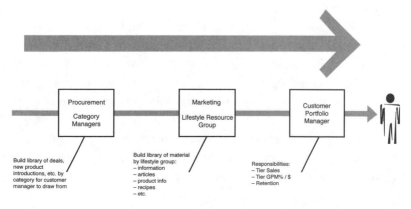

The Customer Portfolio manager has control of some budget for price discounting, gained from revamping the purchasing function to maximize a constant gross profit margin. This budgeted portion of gross margin can now be allocated in the form of price reductions to influence customer behavior, albeit at a more favorable rate of return than traditional retailing in which the same deal price is offered to everyone, including customers that would have purchased the product at regular retail price.

As we can begin to see, the development of a data platform structure combined with existing communication technologies in the form of kiosks, websites, and e-mail, will have profound impact on how retail companies are organized and go to market. These developments also set the stage for new business strategies, altering the traditional rules of engagement retail companies have had to abide by for years.

In an environment where customer specific communication is practical and accepted, a one-price-for-all retail philosophy may no longer offer the strongest return on investment. A retail company operating with an everyday low price strategy is really pricing to the average customer, seeking to strike price points that are strong enough to provide a competitive edge over retail competitors and still maintain a level of profitability. In the new world of retail there is really no such thing as an average consumer. Each customer is an individual, having his or her own motivations relative to products, prices, and shopping experience.

Retailers competing with an everyday low price competitor no longer necessarily have to match the cost structure of their competitor to stay in the game. By getting close on costs, the new retail enterprise can alter the value equation offered the consumer by presenting products and information relevant to the customer at price points that are meaningful enough to drive behavior. By marketing this way, the new retailer can maximize customer yield, and more than make up for a reasonable difference in cost structure. By maximizing customer yield, increasing customer spending and margin, a retailer can achieve greater profitability than a retailer pricing to a customer average.

Let's look to the highly competitive supermarket channel for an example of this strategy, using the battle between Kroger, the largest traditional supermarket company in the U.S., and Wal-Mart as our stage. As has been well documented, Wal-Mart's cost structure is significantly lower than Kroger's, in part because of their everyday low price strategy. For purposes of our illustration, let's assume that Kroger has the systems capability discussed here for one-to-one retailing and has also worked to channel all trade monies into their everyday product cost; thus creating a larger internal gross margin. While our fictional Kroger utilizes customer-focused retailing, it continues to distribute a regular ad flyer, though at far less cost (due to efficiencies realized with overlaying flyer distribution with customer origination), featuring far fewer items, as its primary purpose is to cost effectively attract (new) customers.

Carol Customer (our fictional shopper) chooses between Kroger and Wal-Mart each week for her grocery shopping. Most times Wal-Mart is the winner of the trip due to their low prices, but Kroger wins on the weeks they have her favorite brands on sale (Tide detergent and Coke soda) as Kroger's temporary sale prices beat Wal-Mart's everyday price.

Kroger, being customer intelligent and having a record of Carol Customer's purchasing, learns that she is brand loyal to Tide and Coke and it appears that there is a strong correlation between these items and when she shops at Kroger. Kroger could now channel some of their expanded gross margin into subsidizing or lowering the price of Tide and Coke to Carol Customer on a regular basis, able to extend these special prices only to Carol Customer, not to all consumers. By doing so, Kroger begins to win Carol's business on a more regular basis - to the detriment of Wal-Mart. Additionally, as she does more shopping with Kroger, Carol finds that more and more she is presented with products and brands that appeal to her, almost as if her weekly ad were customized based upon her preferences.

This strategy is made possible by the systems advances we have spoken of in this section. Kroger no longer is forced to play by Wal-Mart's rules, able now to alter the rules of engagement. A new element has been added to the retail value equation: personalization.

While Wal-Mart maintains an advantage with regard to their cost structure versus Kroger, Kroger is able to mitigate some of this advantage through expanding their gross profit margins from the successful practice of customer yield management.

Obviously this is a simplistic example, yet it shows the potential power of a retailer being able to tailor an assortment of products, prices, and information to each individual customer. Similar strategies are possible in any number of retail channels and formats.

The capability of mass retailers to go to market on an individual customer basis will take some time to evolve, but the important first step of systems enabling such a process are here now. Retailers possessing detailed customer information have within their databases the raw material needed to glean the knowledge necessary to understand individual customer's shopping motivations. Green Hills has developed the analysis necessary to learn which specific products engender brand loyalty amongst its thousands of customers. It is only necessary to run such analysis against each customer and category to produce the list of brands relevant to each individual customer.

While some readers may be skeptical of the feasibility of mass retailers going to market in a way suggested here, they should be aware of the availability of the tools enabling this capability.

CONCLUSION

What began with loyalty marketing in retail has come, in a sense, full circle. But with it a view and understanding of retail never before possible. For the first time since the advent of mass retailing it is possible to view and measure all aspects of business, from products to customers, and their profitability and interaction over time.

Much like the recently decoded human genome, customer intelligent retailers can now identify and track all the parts of their business. What is left now is to study the potential combinations, learning the cause and effect of our marketing, advertising, and operational processes on our living, breathing customers.

And just as the rewards will go to the biotech companies who are able to use the newly available tools of the genome map to assemble powerful new drugs, retailers who are able to understand what motivates each individual customer, and then deliver meaningful products, offers, and experience to each customer based upon that learning will have struck shareholder gold.

It is perhaps only a matter of time until customer-based measures find their way to Wall Street. In May 2001 a task force for the Securities and Exchange Commission recommended that companies voluntarily report "intangible assets" to help investors value company stocks. Baruch Lev, an accounting professor at New York University, argues that intangibles such as brands and intellectual property comprise well over half the market value of public companies. Yet financial statements prepared under generally accepted U.S. accounting principles do not provide for the accounting and valuation of these assets. [1]

While it is unlikely there will be a rapid change in accepted accounting principles any time soon, it is likely that some companies will begin to include such measures as part of their statements, particularly if it provides them with advantage amongst analysts. Intangible measures would certainly include customer retention figures, customer acquisition, and a customer inventory. Companies having enough data can readily project future income and profit streams from different customer segments. One of the first movers in this direction is Sprint's PCS wireless division, which in 2002 began reporting customer churn and value, citing them as critical barometers of corporate health. [2] It is reasonable to assume that if Sprint's wireless division is able to document customer retention and customer value numbers superior to their competitors, it will curry them favor with regard to their stock price.

Having been in the retail industry for the past twenty years, I believe that there has never been a time when retail has been more competitive or more exciting, technology at last enabling a profound shift in the traditional business model. Such opportunity presents itself maybe once each generation; to understand the significance of this change in the field of battle and the resulting opportunities related to developing new strategies is vital. Some retail companies, having built their organizations and cultures on a product-centric business model, will be unable to overcome their corporate inertia to fully utilize customer information.

But technology alone will not win the retail battles of tomorrow, just as it has not provided a decisive victory for retailers in the past. Retailing in any channel becomes more competitive by the day, consolidation ever-increasing, channel blur spreading ever-further, and ever-growing numbers of products and retailers becoming commoditized. At the same time, today's consumer has more choices than ever, in products, in retail stores, and in information available.

To compete successfully today requires a retailer do a great many things well, from managing out of stocks to maintaining competitive pricing, from cleanliness of the stores to an acceptable level of customer service. But the companies moving beyond simple survival are disciplined operators, taking full command of the operation of their stores and providing an enjoyable shopping experience for their customers. Such retailers are moving the concept of brand marketing to a new level, in essence branding their stores and the shopping experience provided.

The winners of tomorrow will add customer intelligence to the retail equation, capturing tremendous amounts of accurate customer data and transforming it into knowledge of their customers and using it in how the company goes to market. Availing themselves of new technologies existing today, these pioneers will slowly but surely shift the field of battle from a one-to-many to a one-to-one environment in a mass retail setting.

Welcome to the new world of retail.

END NOTES

Chapter 1:

1. "The Hidden Cost Of Shelf Space", *Business Week*, April 15, 2002, 103.

2. "Borders Sets Out to Make the Book Business Businesslike", *The Wall Street Journal,* May 20, 2002, B1.

3. "Retail Reckoning", *Business Week,* December 10, 2001, 73.

4. "An Update on Retail Consolidation", *Consumer Insight*, A.C. Nielsen, 2000.

5. "An Update on Retail Consolidation", *Consumer Insight*, A.C. Nielsen, 2000.

6. "Canadian Grocer Executive Report", *Rogers Media Publishing*, 2002, 4.

7. "Food Retailing in the 21st Century", *Food Marketing Institute*, 2002, 3.

8. "Consolidation in the Retail Industry", *The Staubach Company*, 2001, 1.

9. "Big Business Can't Swallow These Little Fish", USA Today, March 27, 2002, 1B.

10. "Toys Move Into Supermarkets", The Post-Standard, February 9, 2002, B12.

11. "Next Up: Gas In The Box", *Morningnewsbeat.com*, September 21, 2002.

12. Fred Crawford & Ryan Mathews, *The Myth of Excellence*, (New York, Crown Business, 2001).

13. "Starbucks Signs Deal With Target", "Sharper Image To Build Presence in Circuit City Stores", *Morningnewsbeat.com*, October 11, 2002.

14. "Upscale Discounting at Its Best", *Mass Market Retailers*, 2002, 18.

15. "Levi's Finds It's Hip to be Frugal", *The Post-Standard*, November 3, 2002, E3.

Chapter 2:

1. "A Hard Landing", *Skyguide Go*, Autumn 2002, 16.

2. Brian Woolf, *Loyalty Marketing The Second Act*, (Greenville, Teal Books, 2002), 38.

3. Glen A. Terbeek, *Agentry Agenda*, (Chesterfield, The American Book Company).

4. "Internet Generates Three Million Potential Customers For P&G", *Morningnewsbeat.com,* July 31, 2002.

5. "Dole Doles Out The Green", *Colloquy.com*, June 18, 2002.

6. "Food Industry Trends", *Mass Market Retailers*, May 13, 2002, 29.

7. "Have It Your Way", *USA Today*, October 30, 2002, 3B.

8. "Have It Your Way", *USA Today*, October 30, 2002, 3B.

9. "Prada Previews Retail Technology", *The Post-Standard*, October 29, 2002, C6.

Chapter 4:

1. W. Edwards Deming, *Out of the Crisis* (Cambridge, Massachusetts Institute of Technology, 1986).

2. "Does Loyalty Still Pay", Skyguide, Winter 2003, 21.

Chapter 5:

1. "Questioning Technology's Promises", *Progressive Grocer*, February 1, 2002, 52.

2. "Why and How A Major Supermarket Dropped Its Loyalty Programme", *Thewisemarketer.com*, July 2002.

3. "Home Depot Taps Citigroup to Offer Consumer Credit", *The Wall Street Journal*, May 29, 2002, D2.

4. "Guest Card Bolsters Top Line", *Mass Market Retailers*, May 13, 2002, 65.

5. Visible Results, Auckland, New Zealand, www.visibleresults.com

6. Information gathered discussions with Christie Frazier-Coleman, Vice President of Sales Promotion and Customer Loyalty; Bashas, Phoenix, AZ, United States.

Chapter 6:

1. "The Age of Wal-Mart", *Retailforward.com*, August 14, 2002.

2. Information gathered from data available through the Food Marketing Institute (fmi.org).

3. "Wal-Mart Pressure Begins to Catch Up With Albertsons", *Morningnewsbeat.com*, October 11, 2002.

4. "Can Kroger Win This Food Fight?", Business Courier, September 20, 2002.

5. "Meet Your New Neighborhood Grocer", *Fortune*, May 13, 2002, 94.

6. "Wal-Mart Plans Hundreds Of Neighborhood Markets By 2006", *Morningnewsbeat.com*, April 24, 2002.

7. "Can Kroger Win This Food Fight?", *Business Courier*, September 20, 2002.

Chapter 7:

1. "Japan: Supermarket Launches Targeted Mobile E-Fliers", *Thewisemarketer.com*, December 5, 2001.

2. "Tesco Rolls Out Electronic Coupons", *Thewisemarketer.com*, September 5, 2002.

3. Information gathered through research interviews with Saul Simon, Vice President of Marketing and Business Development, Retalix, Ra'anana, Israel; www.retalix.com.

4. "Sears Consolidates Data Warehouses", *Executive Technology*, June 2002, 48.

5. "Hudson Bay Company", *1to1 Magazine*, January/February 2003, 36.

6. "The Daunting Dilemma of Trade Promotion", Anderson Consulting, 1997.

7. "The Hidden Cost Of Shelf Space", *Business Week*, April 15, 2002, 103.

Conclusion:

1. "Brainpower on the Balance Sheet", *Business Week*, August 26, 2002, 110.

2. "Sprint PCS Wireless Reports Customer Value to Shareholders", *Inside 1to1*, January 21, 2002.

BIBLIOGRAPHY

- Christensen, Clayton M. *The Innovator's Dilemma.* Boston: Harvard Business School Press, 1997.

- Collins, Jim. Good to Great. New York: HarperCollins Publishers, 2001.

- Crawford, Fred and Mathews, Ryan. *The Myth of Excellence.* New York: Crown Business, 2001.

- Deming, W. Edwards. *Out of the Crisis.* Cambridge: Massachusetts Institute of Technology, 1986.

- Kingston, Anne. *The Edible Man.* Toronto: Macfarlane Walter & Ross, 1994.

- Terbeek, Glen A. *Agentry Agenda.* Chesterfield, Breakaway Strategies, Inc.

- Reichheld, Frederick F. *The Loyalty Effect.* Boston: Harvard Business School Press, 1996.

- Ries, Al. *Focus.* New York: HarperCollins Publishers, 1996.

- Treacy, Michael and Wiersema, Fred. *The Discipline of Market Leaders.* Cambridge: Perseus Books, 1995.

- Trout, Jack. *Big Brands Big Trouble.* New York: John Wiley & Sons, Inc., 2001

- Woolf, Brian. *Loyalty Marketing The Second Act.* Greenville: Teal Books, 2002.

In addition to the above works, the following internet based sources and news services were most helpful in providing background material and related information:

www.morningnewsbeat.com

www.thewisemarketer.com

www.inside1to1.com

Hawkins Strategic, LLC
P.O. Box 145
Skaneateles, NY 13152-0145
US 315.685.5282
US 315.685.5283 (fax)
www.hawkinsstrategic.com

INDEX

D

E

F

Friedlander, Gary   129, 149, 151-152

F. W. Dodge   5

G

G., Tom   18

Gap, Inc.   76

Gateway   42

George apparel   14

Giannulli, Mossimo   14

Giant Stores   8-9

Graves, Michael   14

Green Hills   1, 4, 15, 26, 35-36, 38, 69-71, 89-9, 93, 95, 129, 131, 153-156, 167, 184

H

HEB   151

Hergott, Joan   146

Hertz   42-43

Hewlett-Packard   42

Home Depot   8, 13, 116

Hudson Bay Company   176

I

IBM   42

Ikea   8

I.N.C. apparel   14

M

N

O

P

R

S

V

Visa   116

Visible Results   23, 27, 28, 117

Vivero   123-124, 126

Voisin, Greg   132

Voisin, Mac   131, 148

W

Walgreens   8

Wal-Mart   5-9, 13-16, 109, 126, 131, 151, 157-162, 178, 182-183

Wall Street   14, 34, 185

Web Miles   113

Welcome Break Group   176

Wertkauf   7

Whole Foods   151-152

Woolf, Brian   36, 66

Y

Yamamoto, Yasuo   164

Yield management   32-33, 56-57

Z

Zellers   135